Edgar Cayce Revisited

And Other Candid Commentaries

by
Gina Cerminara

The Unilaw Library
Donning
Virginia Beach/Norfolk

Library of Congress Cataloging in Publication Data

Cerminara, Gina
    Edgar Cayce revisited and other candid commentaries.
    1. Cayce, Edgar. 1877-1945—Addresses, essays, lectures. 2. Reincarnation—Addresses, essays, lectures. 3. Psychical research—Addresses, essays, lectures. 4. Cerminara, Gina—Addresses, essays, lectures. I. Title.
BF1027.C3C4   1983   133.8   83-16321
ISBN 0-89865-324-X (pbk.)

Printed in the United States of America

CONTENTS

V

EDITOR'S PREFACE

I have been an ardent admirer of Gina Cerminara since I first read *Many Mansions,* that inspiring and groundbreaking study of the Edgar Cayce material, many years ago. Each of her succeeding books—the two sequels to *Many Mansions, The World Within* and *Many Lives, Many Loves;* her brilliant and innovative book on religion, *Insights for the Age of Aquarius*; and her totally unexpected comic novel, *The Mark Twain Proposition*—has served to deepen my admiration for the breadth of her interests and the versatility of her literary skills.

But, like many other readers and admirers of her books all over the world (she has been translated into eleven languages), I have been curious about her as a person and curious about what other things she may have written that I may have missed.

When I found that she was living in the same town that I was—Virginia Beach, Virginia—I felt impelled to approach her, both to express my profound personal appreciation for her work and tell her how much it had widened the horizons of my thinking, and, as an editor with an ulterior motive in mind, to ask her why it had been so long since she had written a book.

She accepted my homage with modesty (as I had thought she would), and replied to my question by telling me that she had been devoting all her time and energies to an organization which she had founded and been the president of for the previous five years: the Animal Assistance League of Virginia. The exploitation, abuse, and neglect of animals in our society were matters which deeply concerned her, she said. She had recently resigned the presidency, however, because it was becoming increasingly difficult to do justice both to the never-ending demands of humane work and to her heavy schedule of out-of-town lectures.

Sensing a possible new book, perhaps on the subject of animals, I asked her if she had any literary plans. No, she said, not at present.

Undaunted, I asked her if she had published any magazine articles over the years which might be of interest to the readers of her books. Well, yes, she admitted; she had written on a number of topics: a few poems, some travel pieces, a number of articles about psychic things, General Semantics, and animals; but whether or not such a miscellany would interest her readers might be questionable.

On the contrary! I exclaimed. This is just what your readers would like: an opportunity to know you better as a person, to learn something of your history and how you became interested in things and how they affected your life and your work. Why don't you gather them together, write a brief explanatory introduction to each piece, and we'll publish them?

She was reluctant at first; but finally, several telephone conversations later, she agreed to do it. As the project proceeded, she felt moved to write several new pieces, created especially for the collection, including the article from which this book's title is drawn.

I am delighted with the result, and I feel that others will be also. A hundred years from now, scholars of literary history and of the emergence of what is known as the New Age—if, pessimistic note, there are any such scholars one hundred years from now!—will undoubtedly consider this little volume valuable for its many insights into the mind and heart of one of the twentieth century's authentic and seminal literary figures. On the other hand— optimistic note—if civilization survives for another hundred years, it may well be (in part, at least) because Gina Cerminara's books injected so much sanity and so many wholesome and compassionate ideas into the otherwise muddied and violent stream of twentieth-century thinking.

—The Editor

Edgar Cayce Revisited

And Other Candid Commentaries

INTRODUCTION

In every person's life there are certain special events that happen at precisely the right times. Some people, perhaps most, consider these as coincidental and nothing more. I think otherwise.

On March 4, 1970, I was working the night shift as a busboy and dishwasher at Foothill Community College where I attended classes during the day in Los Altos Hills, California. One of the routine duties I performed was to gather the serving trays from the dinner counter, load them on a cart, and take them back to be washed. This is a chore that I had done many times before without incident, but tonight was different. My mind was preoccupied, as it had been for some time, with the idea of suicide. I was contemplating suicide for reasons too complicated to be presented here. I can only say that life had been reduced, for me, into a simple formula: either you get hurt, or you hurt someone else. I wanted no part of such a life, and had already thought out the where and the how of ending it. As I wheeled toward the dishroom, I moved closer to the decision that I would actually do it.

At the exact moment that I made this decision, several stainless steel trays crashed to the floor with such a racket that the hair on the back of my neck stood on end. Simultaneously, I heard what seemed to be a voice in my head telling me that I would really be making a serious mistake if I killed myself. After the initial shock subsided, I said to whoever or whatever it was that spoke to me: "Okay, I won't kill myself, but only on one condition: you have got to give me something to live for."

1

A few days later, I got a phone call from a woman I did not know. The local Heart Fund needed someone to go door-to-door to collect donations. I had never volunteered for anything like this before, so I surprised myself when I said yes.

That evening, after soliciting at all the houses in the court where I lived, and collecting small sums, I decided to try one more house—the pink one adjoining my parents' place, just outside the court, on the corner of Springer Road.

As I approached the pink house I didn't know what to expect, and toyed with the idea of going home; but the magnificent old oak trees on the front edge of the property seemed to welcome me. In fact the whole place had a friendly atmosphere about it. I crossed the circular driveway, accidentally scattering wild bird seed with my foot, took the three or four steps up to the porch, and rang the bell. A woman answered the door. I couldn't remember having met her before, but I liked her instantly. She was of average height, with shoulder length, dark brown hair. The cast of her face was Mediterranean, with a hint of Egyptian nobility, and her eyes shone with an indescribable intelligence.

"Hello," she said, with a bright smile, "What can I do for you?"

I was generally shy with strangers, but she made me feel at ease. I told her that I was collecting for the Heart Fund, and asked if she would care to make a donation.

"I'm sorry," she said, "but I will not contribute to an organization that experiments on animals." I must have looked puzzled because she asked if I had heard of vivisection before. I said that I hadn't, and before I knew it I was sitting on her couch eating protein cookies, drinking fruit juice, and listening attentively as she spoke about the cruelties of animal experimentation.

After three or four hours I found that I had not only been made aware of what was happening to animals in research laboratories, but also of the life of Edgar Cayce, the philosophy of reincarnation and karma, and the benefits of vegetarianism and natural foods. Later, on the way home, I realized that this woman had given me something to live for. She had awakened my mind and given me ideas that were exciting, meaningful, and somehow strangely familiar. I felt exhilarated and reassured, and the thought of suicide became a thing of the past.

It has been thirteen years now since I first met Gina Cerminara on the doorstep of her pink house in Los Altos. In that time I have come to know Gina as not only a gifted writer and lecturer, but as a person who really lives by the principles of compassion and sanity that she writes and lectures about.

Up until I met Gina I had been an "armchair altruist." I talked a lot about being of service in the world, but when it came time to do anything, I just didn't know how.

Gina taught me how.

Knowing Gina has taken me into the workings of The Animal Assistance League of Virginia—an organization dedicated to the rescue, feeding, and adoption of unwanted and neglected animals. The League was founded by Gina and two of her friends in 1976, and as of this writing (1983) is still going strong helping to relieve the suffering of thousands of animals.

Knowing Gina has also taken me into a state penitentiary, a soup kitchen, and many a poor neighborhood, both black and white, where she has gone to teach, serve food, or distribute clothing. Gina has a natural inclination to do charitable work, which reflects the more serious side of her nature, but she has another side which is one of her most notable characteristics—a sense of humor (those who have heard Gina lecture can attest to her effective use of it). But Gina's sense of humor only enhances and brings a sense of balance to the deep concern she has for the problems of this world and of the beings, both human and nonhuman, that live in it.

I am grateful to be able to count myself among the many persons who have been turned around by the books, lectures, and caring friendship of Gina Cerminara.

—John L. Harrison

PART I:
PSYCHIC MATTERS

When people ask me, politely, "How did you get interested in the psychic field?" I sometimes sense undercurrents to the question—especially if it has been asked by an academic person. I cannot help but think of the stock question that (I am told) is frequently asked of ladies of the evening: "How did a nice girl like you get into an occupation like this?" In my case the wonderment seems to be "How did an intelligent person like yourself" or possibly "How did a sensible person like yourself" get involved in so dubious, even so disreputable a field.

I have no pat or simple answer to the question; and, as a matter of fact, if you will stop to think about it, it is not really easy to give a totally simple answer to any such question about the interests and commitments of one's life. "How did you get so interested in bees?" or "Why did you decide to become a dentist?" or "How do you happen to feel such a fascination for the culture of the ancient Mayans?"* really involve both subtle and complex inter-related factors.

In my case, as regards the psychic field, there are a number of basic inter-related reasons to account for my interest; but perhaps the most outstanding is the fact that I had a second cousin in

---

*Totally unnecessary footnote (To be ignored by those who detest atrocious puns): Somebody who introduced himself as an artist once came up to me after a lecture and said: "Did you know that you have a very Mayan profile?" I said, "Really?" "Yes. You really do." "Well," I said, "I'm not so sure I'm happy to know it's really Mayan . . . I have sometimes wished it belonged to somebody else."

Florence, Italy, who had some extraordinary psychic and psycho-kinetic gifts. I never met her or saw her demonstrate her talents, but my mother, grandmother, and other members of her family who lived in Florence at that time had witnessed these manifestations often. Her gifts appeared spontaneously at an early age, much to the distress of her parents, who tried unsuccessfully to suppress them. They were affluent and very orthodox Catholics; they never allowed her to display her talents in public, and accepting money for them would have been unheard of. Naturally the case was frequently discussed in my family and sometimes with visitors who were interested in the subject, and it gave a definite bent to my thinking.

I know a number of professional parapsychologists who have become interested in this field for similar reasons. That is to say, either they themselves have had some inexplicable and unprecedented psychic experience, or some member of their family has.

This interest of mine has led me down many strange pathways. I have known personally many psychics and count many of them as my friends. I have seen how helpful they can be to people, and I have also seen the special difficulties that they face in their own lives. My study of the Edgar Cayce readings with which my name seems to be most usually associated is only one part of this broader interest which has persisted all my life.

PSYCHIC ONE-UP-MANSHIP

I received more reader response from this article—published in the A.R.E. Journal in November 1981—than any other article I've ever written. People from all over the United States wrote me telling me how much they had enjoyed it and how much I had voiced their own feelings and observations. "It's about time somebody said something like this," was a frequent comment. Many others expressed the wish that the article had been longer, or that I would write another one in similar vein. "Now won't you please do one about people who think they give 'readings'!" someone wrote. I am strongly tempted to do just that.

It used to be that you could put other people down and yourself up by the simple method of dropping names ("I met Burt Reynolds last night at a party!") or places ("When I was in Tahiti last summer...").

Names are still good, of course, provided that you can manage to acquire a few authentic ones, but places are not. Now that any number of teen-agers have flown at special rates or gone on exchange programs to distant parts of the globe, and vast numbers of anti-establishmentarians have hitch-hiked or stowed away to ditto ditto, you run the risk in dropping place names of being smartly and smugly topped. "Oh, yes. Tahiti. I was there three years ago."

But, fortunately, there is now emerging a new and very effective method of one-up-manship that, unlike travel, costs no money at all and can be topped only by experts who know the game better than you do. Other ordinary clods can still be mightily

7

impressed. I refer, of course, to the new game of psychic one-up-manship.

This game is played principally at social gatherings, or even in tete-a-tete situations, and it consists in talking about or "demonstrating" the psychic gifts you have and other people do not.

There are several categories. One of the most common is seeing the aura. You are at a party and after studying one of the guests and the ambient air for several moments, you say, knowingly, "Your aura is a lovely pink (or yellow, or gold, or fuchsia) tonight." This neatly accomplishes several things: It shows how psychic you are, and it flatters the recipient in a much more with-it way than: "What gorgeous earrings you're wearing!" or "I love your hair."

There is another ploy which I have heard on several occasions. It goes like this: "My, how dark and muddy your aura is tonight. Aren't you feeling well, dear?" This also shows how psychic you are, but it is, of course, a nasty put-down (especially when said in the presence of other people) and implants negative suggestions in the mind. It is not to be recommended if you believe in karma and if you wish to be thought charming.

Another category of psychic one-up-manship is to be found in the area of psychic healing. The group has decided to sing Findhorn songs, or do Sufi dancing, or chant African chants with drum accompaniment. One of the ladies present does not join in and when asked why, explains that she has a bad headache. You step forward and say, a modest smile playing on your lips, "I'm a good healer. I can cure your headache."

The lady says thank you, but she thinks she ought to go home. You insist, and the hostess insists, and finally, rather than be thought unappreciative, the lady allows herself to be brought into an adjoining room where you proceed to apply your particular brand of psychic healing.

This greatly impresses the group (you think), especially since out of courtesy the lady later says she feels "a little better," though in point of fact she feels considerably worse. It really does not concern you that (1) the lady actually did not have a headache, but preferred to pretend having one rather than get involved with Findhorn singing, Sufi dancing, African chanting, or whatever other noisy esoteric merriment the crowd was getting into; or (2) she really did have a headache but did not especially want a total stranger to lay his hands on her solar plexus or do acupressure on her neck, thereby messing up her hair; or (3) she really did have a headache and wanted nothing more than to get out and go home, *now,* to apply her own method of esoteric or exoteric healing, very likely including two aspirins.

None of these possibilities need concern you because it is far more important (you feel) to be thought a psychic healer than it is to be sensitive to the feelings of other people or aware of each person's right to privacy and freedom from psychic dabbling. At least such seems to be the outlook of many psychic one-up-manship practitioners, who appear to be proliferating in recent years.

Frankly, I am beginning to wish that nobody be allowed to say or do anything "psychic" without being invited to do so, and possibly even without having first gotten some kind of psychic accreditation from a knowledgeable Board of Examiners.

This point of view will make me very unpopular in certain psychic circles, no doubt, but if that be the case, I would just as soon be counted among the squares.

ADVICE TO ASPIRING PARAPSYCHOLOGISTS

For several years Psychic *magazine (which later changed its name to* New Realities) *ran a feature called* Opinion, *for which they invited people in the psychic field to express their views on some topic of their own choosing. In 1973 I was asked to contribute such an article, and the following piece was published in the December 1973 issue.*

Last spring three college students approached me, on separate occasions, with the same question: What should they do to prepare themselves for becoming parapsychologists? My answer was to get as wide a background as possible in psychology, biology, anthropology, biochemistry, physics, and any other branch of science that interested them. Parapsychology is in a way a misnomer; the things that it studies include much more than merely mental processes, normal or paranormal, of human beings. In order to understand the strange and varied phenomena which are already within its scope one needs as broad a base of understanding as possible.

One of the students said to me that his college counselor had strongly advised him against going into parapsychology because the current wave of interest in it was only a passing fad. I was reminded of the learned professor who stated, after the first demonstration of electric light at the Paris Exposition: "I can assure you that when the Paris Exposition closes, electric light will

Reprinted with permission from *Psychic* magazine, 680 Beach St., San Francisco, California 94109

close with it and nothing more will be heard of it again."

In this connection I told the students the story of the snail who was painfully inching his way up the icy trunk of a cherry tree in December. A friendly beetle stuck his head out of a crack and said, "Hey, buddy, you're wasting your time. There aren't any cherries up there!"

The snail kept right on going. "I know, but there will be by the time I get there."

As of now there may not be many fulltime paid openings for parapsychologists in the United States, but—though I am no seeress—I believe I can confidently predict that within the next twenty-five years there will be.

Meanwhile I must confess that my enthusiasm for the upsurge of interest in psi phenomena is not unalloyed. I have reservations. They are similar, in some respects, to the reservations I feel about television. This electronic marvel, this communication miracle of the century, has conferred many benefits upon mankind: entertainment, information, exposure to sights and sounds and manners and products and people that otherwise would never have been known. But it is also being used to propagate vulgarities without number, inanities like unto the sands of the sea, and all too many blatant untruths or subtle half-truths by certain advertising interests. The new mode of communication carries with it no built-in protection against misuse.

Nor do the new-old modes of communication called telepathy and clairvoyance. They, too, can be used constructively, and already have been in medicine, education, psychological counseling, police work, and scientific research. But they can also be used to invade privacy, pirate ideas, manipulate others, control the lives of the less able and the less clever.

A study of the advertisements in certain psychic publications results almost inevitably in the conclusion that the populace is still motivated by self-interest and the drive to power. "Control others with your mind! Send $5.00 for fascinating course in psychic powers. Money refunded if not completely thrilled." "Know what others are thinking! Learn how to project your mind. Influence men and women to do what you want them to do."

Expensive courses in developing ESP are becoming increasingly popular all over the country. In some of them one is required to sign a pledge that one will use whatever psychic abilities one develops only for good and constructive purposes. This pledge is a manifestation no doubt of the good intent of those who give the

11

courses and is very probably taken seriously by many who sign it. But somehow I feel it is unrealistic to believe that the signing of pledges invariably confers instant integrity, and that people who are unstable, neurotic, immature, or malevolent will be any less so after obtaining psychic powers than they were before.

To achieve the communication skills of telepathy or clairvoyance is not automatically accompanied by kindness, discretion, and spiritual maturity, any more than to achieve the skills of typing or shorthand would be. I have known a goodly number of psychically talented people who patently were using their gift for self-inflation (hardly anything can match the heady feeling of being regarded omniscient) or to enrich their bank balances or to meddle, on occasion, in the lives of others.

Any step forward in psi powers must be accompanied, I am convinced, by an equal step forward ethically and spiritually. Every new power of the mind must be matched by a new power of the heart; by compassion and concern for all forms of life. Otherwise the psychic revolution could well become a disastrous component of the debacle of our civilization.

These considerations led me to add some final words of counsel to the college students who wanted to be parapsychologists: Whether the goal is to be a researcher or a teacher in the field, I believe it is essential for a parapsychologist to be knowledgeable not only in several sciences but also in the fields of literature, ethics, General Semantics, comparative religion, and whatever spiritual and meditational disciplines that appeal to them in order to improve their state of being.

I believe it would be well for them also to spend at least a year in some form of disciplined social service, coming directly to grips with the complicated problems that beset people. Too many of our scientists and researchers have been narrow and materialistic in their intellectuality, as well as emotionally stunted and socially myopic. Our tragic planetary situation is due, I believe, at least in part to their pervasive influence.

I would like to see parapsychologists be a new breed of scientist: TOTAL human beings, well-balanced emotionally, well-grounded ethically and spiritually, and with true human concern. By the very nature of their data, parapsychologists are uniquely equipped to help create a new world civilization, founded on a new and more spiritual concept of reality. In this respect they could well regard their life work as a mission comparable to that of spiritual leader or priest, who, in the finest sense of that term, is one who helps build a bridge for people from the lower frequencies of material existence to the higher ones of non-material principles and forces, and one who teaches people of the spiritual realities of the universe.

ON THIS DIET EAT EVERYTHING— JUST DON'T SWALLOW

A high school boy, asked to write something about Socrates, once wrote: "Socrates was a Greek. He went around lecturing people. They poisoned him."

I often think of this wry bit of historical reporting when I am invited to lecture, and often feel that lecturing people, if not necessarily a dangerous occupation, is probably a futile one. None the less I continue to lecture, simply because I enjoy it and because I still cherish the hope, or perhaps illusion, that people do remember something of what one says and find it useful.

The following article is essentially the subject matter of a talk I have given frequently in recent years.

A number of years ago I saw a cartoon that showed a rather stout lady in a doctor's office. The doctor was saying: "Now on this diet you can eat *everything.* Just don't swallow."

What with a new diet system coming out every other week or so, keeping their originators and their publishers very well fed indeed, this little capsule diet system struck me as being both timely and original. Perhaps it shouldn't be taken literally by people who want to get thinner; but it certainly could be taken to heart metaphorically at least by those who wish to keep their sanity in a world going madder every day. "Read everything you wish," I would paraphrase it, "but don't believe everything you read." "Listen to anybody you want to; but don't swallow everything you hear!"

The advice is apropos with regard to practically every piece of communication one might happen to be exposed to—whether it be a newspaper or magazine article, a book, a lecture, a conversation, or a TV commercial. One should always listen or read with a filter around one's head, so to speak: a filter for separating what one can reasonably accept and what one should reasonably be cautious of accepting.

The filter of discrimination is particularly necessary, I think, in regard to the whole field of the psychic.

We are living in an age that has been aptly called the Age of Anxiety; and it is hardly necessary to spell out the reasons why.* Many people are frightened, confused, depressed, and anxious. It is no wonder that they are often attracted to the whole fascinating field of the psychic, or to the personal advice of psychics.

I personally have no quarrel with this attraction. I do not feel with the materialistic and academic psychologist that the whole psychic field is illusory, and beneath serious consideration. Nor do I feel with the fundamentalists that psychics are "tools of the devil." I know from much observation that psychics can be enormously helpful, both as personal counselors and as consultants in such technical areas as crime detection, archeological research, and medical diagnosis.

The problem is, though, that some of those who seek out psychic information are often gullible. This is so true that I have for a long time been thinking of writing a book about it called *Gullible's Travels.*

Gullibility, of course, can be found in many places besides the field of the psychic. I have a sizeable collection of examples—including one of a German traveling salesman who was fined $17 in Koblenz, Germany, for selling "intelligence pills" to parents of children doing badly in school. He sold pills at $25 a box, claiming they were a guaranteed cure for stupidity. Some parents complained to the police when the pills failed to work....

The examples of human gullibility that one might cite are so numerous, in fact, that twenty volumes could not exhaust them. They are a product partly of stupidity, partly of inexperience, partly of lack of information, partly of suggestibility, and partly of the readiness of some people to take shrewd advantage of these weaknesses in others.

---

*Frightening Footnote. Even in our own homes, that last citadel of security, we seem not to be safe any more. A recent book entitled *Why Your House May Endanger Your Health* spells out the very real dangers of floor wax, wallpaper, high pile rugs, lead-based paints, and lead-soldered water pipes, to mention only a few of the chemically-derived conveniences which we tend to use without question. Written by Alfred V. Zann, M.D., with Robert Gannon; Simon and Schuster, N.Y., 1980.

Gullibility regarding psychic matters is due to precisely the same weaknesses, but it is complicated by the fact that psychics are held in special esteem by those who believe in them. There is a halo of infallibility about them, so to speak, much as there is a halo of infallibility about medical doctors for those who believe in orthodox medicine.*

On the basis of my own investigations into the field, I would like to submit a few inter-related propositions that can be helpful to anyone who is interested in obtaining psychic advice. These are as follows:

Proposition 1: The psychic gift exists on a scale which can be roughly calibrated as poor, mediocre, good, excellent, superior. Below the zero end of the scale are the out-and-out frauds, of which there are a goodly number.

Proposition 2: Even the best psychics are inaccurate part of the time, an 85% accuracy rate being very commendable.

Proposition 3: All psychics, even an excellent or superior one, can have a bad session, a bad day, a bad week, or a bad month for reasons of fatigue, poor health, or psychological stress.

Proposition 4: Psychics sometimes lapse into personal or normal observations when they do not get any genuinely psychic impressions. This is often done unconsciously and innocently enough; but if persistently and consciously done during periods when they are not functioning well psychically, could rightly be called "faking it."

Proposition 5: Even the best of psychics can lose their gift completely, yet continue working by "faking it." The faking happens because of two major reasons:

Proposition 6: Psychics, like other human beings, usually need to earn their own living; and even when this need is not urgent or crucial, they can be prompted, like anybody else, by the desire for money.

Proposition 7: Psychics, like other people, can be motivated by ego drives, or the desire for power, or the need to appear in a favorable light. They sometimes do not wish to lose face by admitting that their psychic gift is not functioning, or has disappeared entirely.

There is probably no need to elaborate on any of these propositions, which usually seem pretty understandable to a

---

*As opposed to those who have become disenchanted, or those interested in nutritional, naturopathic, or holistic approaches. See an illuminating volume by Dr. Robert Mendelssohn, *Confessions of a Medical Heretic.*

thinking person once they have been brought to his or her attention. But it may be worth while to elaborate upon propositions 6 and 7, concerning the motivations of psychics. The desire for money and the desire for power or ego satisfaction need to be carefully considered because they relate subtly but importantly to the possible reliability of the information that is given.

A psychic counselor, like any other counselor, can be regarded as a member of the so-called helping professions. I would say that most of the professional psychics I have encountered were genuinely motivated by the desire to help people. But I have come to see that the desire to be helpful, like any other genuine human motivation, can be mixed at the very outset with baser human elements, such as the desire to impress others or the desire to seem superior and infallible, or it can be corrupted in the passage of time to something quite self-seeking.

One unusual instance of ego motivation came to my attention a few years ago. It was told to me by the dean of the Department of Humanities of a certain college where I had been invited to give a course on parapsychology.

The dean was completely sympathetic to this field, but he had seen instances of psychic misuse which were in part what prompted him to authorize a course in the subject. He related this episode to me.

A young male student in one of his classes began to get the reputation of being psychic. He could do amazing things, such as tell a person his social security number, or the date of his birth, or the name and address of a distant friend, or other precise information that would be relatively inaccessible to a stranger or a casual acquaintance. He was also beginning to give "readings" to people with advice about the present and predictions about the future. Several students found reason to be suspicious of him and began to speculate that he might be obtaining his precise data by other than psychic means.

They decided to set a trap for him by placing a sheet of false information about a fellow-student on the desk in the dean's office at a time when it was know that he (the suspected student) would be alone there. (Occasionally he did some secretarial work for the dean.) Later, when he related this invented information as if it were psychic to the student in question, they reported it to the dean, who called the student into his office and confronted him with what had happened.

The young man confessed with some embarrassment that he really was not psychic, and that he had a photographic memory.

Whenever he was in a cafeteria line (for example) and a student in front of him opened a wallet or purse, he would look at whatever private cards or papers were visible, imprint the information on them in his mind, and regurgitate it as if psychic later. He sometimes had access to student papers and records in the dean's office, and again would absorb personal data in the same way. His "readings" about the present and future were either partly based on the data he picked up in this manner (the correctness of which gave him credibility) or were pure fabrication.

The interesting point of this story is this: the young man had no need for money. He came from a very affluent family. But he was obese and unprepossessing in appearance; he had a very poor self-image; he was not popular. Being "psychic" gave him a sense of importance and acceptance, and it did not trouble him at all that the "predictions" and advice he was giving people could have been very misleading and sometimes downright dangerous. Here we have a clear-cut case of fraud, even though money was never involved.

I know another case, that of a businessman who may have had some slight psychic faculty, but who also had the overwhelming need to be regarded as psychic. He would approach people who, he knew, had some interest in psychic things, take them by the hand, look into their eyes, and, without invitation, give them some "impressions" or "predictions." They were often of a negative sort, and I remember an agonized phone call from a woman I knew to whom he had given one such "impression" which had left her in a state of depression for weeks. It was of such a personal nature that she would not even tell me what he said; but it required half a dozen phone calls and innumerable reassurances not to believe what he said, and why not, before her depression lifted.

These are instances of totally or almost totally non-psychic people who can do immeasurable harm to impressionable people by their fabrications, and whose motivation is clearly not that of money but rather that of a sense of personal power.

But money is the motivating force in many other cases. In Brazil, a country in which psychic beliefs and practices are very prevalent, the money motive is virtually non-existent among psychics. The philosophy of Alan Kardec, whose books *The Book of the Mediums* and *The Book of the Spirits* could be called the Bibles of Brazilian Spiritism, insists on charity as the most necessary attribute of Christian living and expressly forbids the taking of money for psychic or spiritual gifts.* Donations may be accepted, but are never asked for. Even a lecturer on spiritual matters is not

18

expected to charge for his services—a fact which I discovered when I began to make plans for a tour of Brazil.

But in other parts of the world, including the United States, most psychics earn their living by using their psychic gifts. The implications of this practice (whatever its ethics might be) are of considerable importance.

Flagrant abuses of psychic talent or pretended talent for financial gain are very frequent. Here is a case I read about in *The Milwaukee Journal*. It concerned a twenty-four-year-old university student who had recently inherited a large sum of money. One day, driving down the streets of Madison, Wisconsin, she saw the sign of a palmist called "Mother Ann." The girl dropped in for a consultation and was impressed by the number of accurate statements Mother Ann made about her. Among other things she was told that the money she had inherited carried an evil curse which the palmist said she could remove for a certain fee. (The newspaper article did not make clear whether Mother Ann psychically perceived the inheritance, or the girl told her about it. My suspicion is that the girl told her about it—very probably in the naive hope of being told what to do with it.) The girl agreed to pay the fee, and kept returning to Mother Ann for further advice, only to learn that the curse was a really heavy one and more money was needed to remove it. Finally she had given Mother Ann $62,000— and then Mother Ann disappeared, leaving no trace behind her. The girl went to the police, who in all probability were never able to apprehend the palmist or restore the girl's money.

Mother Ann may really have had some psychic talent. Palmistry can in some cases be as good a focus as any other for receiving psychic impressions. The probability is high, however, that the college student, like many other inexperienced people, unwittingly fed data to the palmist without realizing what she was doing, or that the palmist, being a shrewd practical psychologist, made observations (of the girl's car, her dress, her speech, her facial expressions, her mannerisms, etc.) which enabled her to say things of seeming psychic validity.

Anyone who doubts the extent to which the cold-blooded abuse of the name of psychic or medium can be put should read a book called *The Psychic Mafia*—the true confessions of a fraudulent

---

*It could be argued that in a sense, almost all talents are spiritual gifts, and should not be charged for, in which case we might have to go back to a system of barter. It can also be argued that a psychic is not charging for his spiritual gift, but for his time—which is not an inconsiderable item. However, these and other arguments are not our concern at the moment.

medium named Lamar Keene. In a chapter entitled "Secrets of the Seance," Keene reveals some of the methods he used to obtain information on people before a seance began. Unlike the college student just described who relied on a photographic memory, Keene used such brazen methods as having an assistant pilfer purses and billfolds in a darkened seance room before the seance began (later returning them with equal deftness without anyone being the wiser), and using an electronic sound collector—a device for picking up conversations at a considerable distance—strategically placed across the street from the Spiritualist Church to collect bits of personal information which were later woven into "messages" from the dead with dramatic and convincing effect. These are only two of dozens of devious methods used by Keene, and according to him, most other fraudulent mediums, to achieve their effects and to harvest millions of dollars from an all too believing public.

It is important, as Rev. Canon William Rauscher* points out in a foreword to Keene's book, to realize that there are *genuine* psychics and mediums as well as fraudulent ones, and that Keene's revelations do not discredit those who *are* genuine. But Keene's personal confessions do show the lengths to which cunning people will go to defraud others. Lamar Keene came to experience a sense of shame and an awakening of conscience, realizing that people were coming to him for "advice in marital, legal, medical, and other problems of their lives," building "their existence here and the hope of a future one on a mere magician's bag of tricks." He finally walked away from the whole sordid scene, never to return to it. But there are hundreds of others who still continue using the same bag of tricks, despite this and other equally shocking exposes.

The misuse of psychic talent (or absence of talent) for money is not always as flagrant and shameless as in the cases of Mother Ann and Lamar Keene. But it is prevalent in other minor ways and many people are given a mixture of psychic perception and psychic nonsense. Sometimes the nonsense causes no harm. In fact, if it consists of psychic flattery it can lead to a temporary state of elation. But spending anywhere from $25 to $1,000 (yes, $1,000!) for a reading that consists of such a mixture is rather like spending 41¢ for a small can of cat food labeled "tuna" or "chicken and

---

*Former president of the Spiritual Frontiers Fellowship and author of *The Spiritual Frontier; The Case Against Suicide;* and with Allen Spraggett, *Arthur Ford, The Man Who Talked With the Dead.*

giblets" and later realizing that the actual contents of the can is 30 percent water.

The anomymous author of *The Boy Who Saw True*,* the autobiography in diary form of a mid-Victorian clairvoyant whose gift developed early in life and who was much misunderstood by his parents and teachers, writes a very interesting passage in one of the last entries in his diary:

"Mrs. S_____ had been worrying me for a long time to go with her to see Mr. _____. Well, yesterday we went and had a 'sitting.' . . . The man is half genuine and half a fraud. When he can't see anything much he invents the most absurd 'psychic compliments.' He told Mrs. S_____ that she had some wonderful occult symbols about her, that she was a very advanced soul, and that she'd soon be going through an important initiation. All rubbish. I could see none of the symbols, and as for her being a very advanced soul, she is nothing of the kind. Quite a decent old sort, but that is all one can say. . .As soon as psychism is mixed up with earning a living that is the sort of thing one gets. You know the Latin adage: 'No man can be wise at all hours of the day'—well, still less can a man be psychic at all hours of the day; the conditions are not always favorable. I don't of course say that all professional psychics are humbugs; far from it. I have known one or two who have been honest enough to say: 'There's nothing around you at the moment," or 'I'm not in form. Better come some other time when conditions are better.'

Reading the autobiographies of professional psychics, especially frank ones, like *The Boy Who Saw True* and Ronald Edwin's *Clock Without Hands,* gives us considerable insight into the problems that genuine psychics face. They are regarded as freaks or frauds by one segment of the population, and venerated as nearly infallible oracles by another. The psychological stresses that must accompany these contradictions, plus the moral stresses of reconciling a talent that is mercurial at best, with the need to earn a living, should cause the rest of us to feel some sympathy with their situation when we find them to be less than angelic.

At the same time, even with all the sympathetic insight we can muster, those of us who consult psychics need to be aware of how we can be duped or at least misled, so that we can be less

---

*Edited by Cyril Scott, Peter Nevill, Ltd., publisher, London, 1953, p. 233.

vulnerable.

Many Americans have read a book called *Autobiography of a Yogi,* and know its author's yogic name: Paramahansa Yogananda. Most of them probably do not know that Paramahansa—like Mahatma—is not a name, like Robert or Frederick, but a title. Mahatma comes from *Maha,* great, and *Atman,* soul, and therefore means *great soul*—a term applied to Gandhi not by himself, but by his worshipful admirers. *Parama* means highest or most perfect; and *Hansa* means swan; therefore: the most perfect swan. This refers to an ancient Hindu legend about a swan who was so marvelously discriminating that he could put his long beak into a pitcher containing a mixture of milk and water, and extract the milk, leaving the water. . . .

In Hindu philosophy, discrimination is a very important virtue: discrimination between the real and the unreal, the eternal and the evanescent, the true and the false.

In this whole slippery psychic field, I submit that discrimination is a virtue we all need to cultivate; and a good symbol for us all to remember would be the Great Swan.

But if the Great Swan seems too exotic a symbol, let us simply recall instead the fat lady in the doctor's office. *On this diet, eat everything. Just don't swallow.*

CAYCE REVISITED

In 1971 Harper & Row published a book by Hugh Lynn and Edgar Evans Cayce, Edgar Cayce's two sons, called The Outer Limits Of Edgar Cayce's Power.

It was a frank and undefensive examination of the instances in which Edgar Cayce's clairvoyance was apparently not successful. It included, for instance, two instances in which he failed to locate a missing child, one of them the famous case of the kidnapped Lindbergh baby. It also included his failures in locating buried treasure and oil wells,* and the instance in which he gave a reading on a person who had died since the time the reading had been requested, and he made no mention of the fact of death.**

In all these instances it was not the intent of the authors to discredit their father, whose phenomenal gifts they had observed at close range for close to forty-three years, but rather to examine the factors involved in the accuracy of psychic data.

It is interesting to note that this book never went into a second printing and was probably the least successful of all the many books written about Cayce. What moral can be drawn from this is not totally clear to me, but I can hazard a few guesses: (1) that people prefer success stories to failure stories; (2) the general public, including Cayce followers, are not particularly

---

*After these failures, Cayce refused to give readings of this kind, feeling that it was not an appropriate use of his gift. His major concern had always been in helping people who were sick.

**It was a complicated situation. The reading was requested on October 7, 1929 for a women who was seriously ill, by her sister-in-law—not by herself. Because of the pressure of many urgent readings for people in the Cayce hospital, which at that time was in operation, Cayce was unable to get to the reading until October 30. In the meanwhile, the woman had died. It is possible that Cayce was tuning in on her condition at the time of the request.

interested in an analysis of the complexities of psychic ability, and the many obscure factors which can interfere with its best performance; and (3) many people who accept a body of psychic data want to believe that the psychic is omniscient. To point out clear-cut instances of error is probably like pointing out to a fundamentalist that there are a number of passages in the Bible which scholars know are false, inaccurate, interpolated, or contradictory. The mind of the fundamentalist simply rejects these facts and encloses itself in the comfortable cocoon of absolute rightness.

The article which follows is the substance of a lecture I have been giving in recent years, mostly to A.R.E. audiences.

Eat everything. Just don't swallow!" is a good watchword not only when we listen to psychic information given us in a private reading, but also when we approach general bodies of psychically derived information.

A surprising number of published books have been written on the basis of psychic sources. The works of Patience Worth are one interesting example. Patience Worth was a seventeen-year-old girl, presumably killed by Indians in early America, and presumably the disembodied author of a long stream of conversations, maxims, poetry, witticisms, and novels on a wide range of subjects. They were produced through the mediumship of Mrs. John Curran of St. Louis, in the early decades of this century. Several of the more than 3,000 poems which she psychically dictated were reprinted in a standard literary anthology, the editor of which was apparently ignorant of the other-worldly character of Patience Worth since he once sent her an invitation to a literary tea in New York!

An earlier and equally impressive example was the work of Alan Kardek—pseudonym of a French mathematician, educator, and intellectual named Hypolyte Rivail (1804-1869) who transcribed a number of books from mediumistic sources. The principal ones were *The Book of the Spirits* and *The Book of the Mediums,* and they consisted of detailed and highly intelligent answers to philosophic and psychic questions. They have become the foundation for the Spiritist movement in France and, surprisingly, in Brazil as well. In that South American country, in fact, virtually half the population espouses Spiritism, which includes a firm belief in spirit communication, spirit healing, and (unlike many British and American Spiritualists) reincarnation as well.

In contemporary America, many other books have been produced by automatic writing, automatic typing, telepathic attunement, and other types of psychic receptivity. Large organizations have been formed on the basis of some of these books, or in some instances, a network of study groups have come into being

24

where enough devoted followers live close together.

I have read many of these productions with interest, and have found in them much that is helpful and seemingly valid. But I have also found some things which I felt questionable, absurd, or downright mischievous.

It is very tempting to discuss my reservations, fully and specifically, about these various psychic revelations, naming the names of the books and citing the passages in question. But to do the subject justice would require a long and carefully documented volume, plus nerves of steel and the fearlessness of a Bengal tiger to meet the True Believers afterwards.

I do not have the time at present to undertake such a book, and am saving whatever fearlessness I have for other matters. So I shall limit my remarks in this article to only one such psychic source, and only one aspect of that.

But before I enter into specifics, I would like to raise a few general questions. First: Why do people tend to believe uncritically anything—psychic or not—that they see in print? A person can lie in print as easily as he can lie in person; or, if the word *lie* seems too harsh, let us say that a person can invent something, and pass it off as fact. . . . I know a writer, now deceased, who casually admitted to me that he had invented a psychic story about a famous poet and included it in one of his published works. I was appalled. Another important consideration: a person may not be willfuly deceptive, but he can, in writing just as easily as in conversation, be mistaken, or confused, or biased. He can be seeing things through the filter of his own limited experience, or his own ignorance. For all these reasons the abject acceptance of things just because they are in print can be sheer folly. I believe that a child's education is incomplete unless it includes training in the critical evaluation of the written word.

But beyond the general tendency toward reverence for the printed word that is still prevalent, despite modern sophistication, there are additional tendencies, purely in the psychic field, to which I would address these questions:

Why do people assume that a psychic source is necessarily always right? Or that a psychic transcription is always totally reliable? And why must *anything* be accepted *totally*?

To those who assume that a psychic source is always right, I would want to say: Only God knows All. To those who believe that the source that is giving them their information is, in fact, God, I would want to say: Maybe so, but remember that He/She is coming through a human transmitter, which is fallible. And to those who

25

believe that something psychic must be accepted totally—in effect, those whose attitude is Every Word Of This Book Must Be True—I would want to say: How is it that you can be discriminating in other areas of your life and not in this one? Many people can go to a movie and say afterwards: "The acting was great! The music was excellent! But the final scene was far too long." Or they can go to a restaurant and say: "It was a marvelous dinner! Everything was perfect except the broccoli. It was soggy." Yet these same people come to their current Psychically Received Bible of Information and they feel it somehow threatening to their newfound sense of security to hear that something in it really doesn't quite compute. Or perhaps they feel that it is an insult to the presumed source of the information—sometimes, supposedly, Jesus, or sometimes simply called, reverentially, the Source, usually implying God.

Whatever the psychological reasons for their unswerving belief in the total truth of their Book, and every sentence in it, the fact remains that such unquestioning devotion can be hazardous to their health.

And this leads me to the specific case on which I wish to dwell, namely the Edgar Cayce information.

This information is vast and varied and has been written about in dozens of books. It covers data on past civilizations, such as Atlantis and Lemuria; biblical history; reincarnation; meditation; and unorthodox methods of healing, to mention only the principal ones. Some of this data (such as the data on Atlantis, Lemuria, and most of the biblical information) cannot be verified: at least not at present. Some of it, such as the information on the Essene community on the shores of the Dead Sea was dramatically confirmed in 1947 by the discovery of the Dead Sea Scrolls. Some of it, such as the meditation instructions, can be, and has been, confirmed experientially in the lives of many people. And some of it, such as the data on physical healing, has been validated thousands of times in the cure not only of the people for whom the original readings were given, but also of people who have applied the same methods since then and have been helped by them. Cayce's recommendations for epilepsy and psoriasis are two of the most outstanding examples of unorthodox treatments that have been highly efficacious, even today. In addition, Cayce was a pioneer in the holistic health movement, emphasizing as long ago as the 1920s that health was a composite of physical, mental, emotional, and spiritual factors, and indicating also that stress was an important factor in many diseases.

So my reservations are not those of a stubborn skeptic or a

hostile critic, and they are not by any means total. They are only partial. They concern several things, but principally they concern diet and health; and they lie (1) partly in a few things that he said, (2) partly in a few things he did not say; and (3) partly in the fact that he said them, or did not say them, many years ago.

It must be remembered that Cayce gave his first reading in the unconscious state on himself, in 1909. Though the subsequent readings, given on himself and others, were usually recorded by stenographers or court reporters, it was not until 1923 that these recorded readings were preserved. He gave his last reading for a person who requested it in July of 1944, and his last reading on himself in September of 1944. As of this writing (1983), then, we are dealing with data that at the very least is thirty-nine years old, and can be as much as sixty years old. It seems hardly necessary to point out that the world has changed greatly in that period of time, and that almost anything suggested that long ago needs to be carefully scrutinized. I would not make an issue of the matter were it not for the fact that I have encountered innumerable Cayce followers to whom this simple fact seems never to have occurred, and who limit their inquiry and their life style to nothing but Cayce data.

First let us consider an example of something he said that needs to be carefully looked at. He often made the general statement: "Coffee is a food." In other instances he qualified the statement by saying: "Coffee, taken properly, is a food—taken, that is, without cream or milk." (Readings 303-P, 303-P-1, 404-P-5, 294-P-37.) On the strength of this rather surprising and rather emphatic statement—which is often quoted in Cayce booklets— many Cayce followers have foregone the use of cream or milk in their coffee, and have felt safe in drinking whatever amounts of coffee they wished.

Many recent medical and scientific studies have indicated that coffee drinking can be highly dangerous. It has been implicated in many psychological problems, including restlessness, worry, fatigue, agitation, depression, and even psychotic behavior. But more ominous is the fact that coffee has also been implicated in such serious physical conditions as ulcers, kidney disease, peri-dontal bone loss (wobbly teeth), gastro-intestinal ailments, heart disease, and cancer.* Women have been sharply warned against drinking coffee during pregnancy, because the caffeine content can

---

*See *The Saturday Evening Post* for June 1982, "Are You a Caffeine Addict?", p. 50-53 and the *Journal of Orthomolecular Psychiatry,* Vol. 10, No. 3, 1981 Series.

cause severe birth defects.*

Dr. Norman Shealy,** a neurosurgeon and a specialist in pain reduction, author of several books and frequent lecturer at the A.R.E., has said that in his considered medical opinion, one or two cups of coffee a day will not harm most people, *unless* they have many other bad chemical habits such as sugar, nicotine, or alcohol. If they have a family history of diabetes or heart disease, the maximum should be one cup a day. But nobody should have more than two cups a day. Contemporary medical opinions of the same sort could be multiplied.

Can we rely, then, on Cayce's statement, qualified only by "taken properly, that is, without cream or milk" that coffee is a food?

I don't think so.

Can we find some explanation for this seeming serious error? Possibly.

It may be that because of the way in which coffee is being grown today, with world-wide pollutants in the air, and with the use of insecticides, sprays, and chemical fertilizers, the quality of the coffee bean has been seriously affected. It may be that the decaffeinating process has a chemical effect which is inimical to human health. It may be that when coffee is made with polluted, fluoridated, or otherwise chemically treated water, its nutritional value is totally invalidated or corrupted. Or it may be that coffee drinking in the excessive and compulsive amounts most people indulge in nowadays exceeds the moderate limits which Cayce may have had in mind, but did not spell out in very explicit terms.

With all these considerations to think of, we need to realize that the statement: "Coffee is a food" can no longer safely be quoted without a number of qualifications. Rather we should say: "Coffee *was* a food at one time," or "Coffee could be a food." And Cayce devotees would be wise not to feel that they are somehow divinely sanctioned and protected in drinking all the coffee they want, just because Cayce said what he did forty, fifty, and sixty years ago.

Similar possibilities must be considered with regard to things

---

* More than twenty scientific studies since 1964 have established the danger of birth defects in laboratory animals that are fed caffeine. The Center for Science in the Public Interest has petitioned the FDA to require a warning label on coffee and tea, warning pregnant women that caffeine may cause birth defects and other reproductive problems (*The Ledger-Star* (Norfolk) April 2, 1980).

** Director of the Shealy Institute of Pain and Health Rehabilitation of Springfield, Mo., and author of *90 Days To Self-Health; Occult Medicine Can Save Your Life; The Pain Game.*

that Cayce said about cigarettes.

Cayce was born in a tobacco-growing state, Kentucky, and grew up "on a tobacco patch," as he often said. He began to smoke when he was quite young and was a chain smoker all his life. Like some of the old Greek philosophers, Cayce was a strong advocate of moderation in all things (though he himself did not always practice it); and he often told people that it was all right to smoke cigarettes as long as they did so in moderation. In fact he went so far as to say that "smoking in moderation to most bodies is helpful. To this body, an excess is harmful, but moderation is not harmful" (Reading 422-2). In some cases he clarified what he meant by moderation. For example: "In moderation it is not harmful, but never smoke more than ten in one day" (Reading 555-11). In another reading he said that five to fifteen to twenty would be "moderate, provided they are smoked far enough apart" (Question 7, Reading 920-2).

Apparently on the strength of statements such as these, many Cayce devotees continue to smoke, many of them—losing sight of the key word, *moderation*—heavily. What they may not have thought about is that at the time when Cayce was giving readings, tobacco was produced in a simpler and more natural way than it is at present. Cayce seemed to be aware of the importance of unprocessed tobacco, because once, having lunch with Harold Reilly, the physio-therapist, he "took out a package of cigarettes, lit one, and drew deeply on it, obviously inhaling," Reilly wrote.* "He must have caught my look of disapproval and surprise, for he said, a little apologetically, 'It's the natural leaf.'" And in a number of readings he indicated that the natural leaf is preferable to the combinations ordinarily found in packaged cigarettes, or the ones that are toasted (Readings 3030-P-16, 1131-P-2, 462-P-3, etc.).

It is important to realize that at present, arsenic and lead sprays are widely used on tobacco plants to repel insects— substances, both of them, that are highly dangerous to human health. Their residues may be small, but cumulative.

Walter S. Ross, editor of *World Smoking And Health,* an American Cancer Society journal, states flatly: *"There is no Healthful amount of smoking. Even a single cigarette is hazardous."* (Emphasis mine.) He substantiates this statement** by explaining

---

The Edgar Cayce Handbook for Health, Dr. Harold J. Reilly, Macmillan, Publisher, 1975, p. 20.

**See "What's Been Added to Your Cigarette?" by Walter S. Ross, *Reader's Digest,* July 1982, P. 111-114.

that at the present time, manufacturers are adding flavors and fragrances to compensate for the reduction of taste and body that follows the reduction of tar. Many of these substances may be made from compounds considered safe for humans, but they are *not* safe when burned. Some of the compounds used are definitely known to be cancer-producing; others are highly suspicious. They include such chemicals as coumarin (once forbidden by the FDA but now being used again), caramel, invert sugar, eugenol, guaical, anglica-root extract, licorice, etc., etc., etc. In the light of this current information, it would seem to me, at least, that any person who continues to smoke, believing that Cayce's statements about smoking in moderation can be relied on, is courting trouble.

Let me now cite an example of something Cayce did *not* say—or at least did not say emphatically enough. I refer to the dangers of sugar.

The case against sugar is so well documented and so shocking that it can well be considered of crucial importance to anyone who values his health or the health of mankind. It is generally known, of course, though for the most part ignored, that sugar is the principal villain in cavities and other disorders of the teeth; but, while mountains of evidence exist, it is not generally known that many degenerative diseases such as cancer, polio, and arthritis are sugar-related or sugar-induced. This is largely because sugar is a chemically refined non-food which not only gives no real nourishment but also leeches important minerals and vitamins from the body. This is not the place to present all the evidence—it would take far too much space; but for those who wish to pursue the matter, perhaps the best place to start is with William Dufty's magnificently researched and readable book, *Sugar Blues*.

It is true, of course, that Cayce frequently told people to stay away completely from sweets, including cake, pie, and candy, or to eat them in moderation. But it is puzzling why he made such a point of saying that beet sugar was superior to cane sugar, without ever explaining why; nor do I know of any current evidence that would substantiate the point, or make the distinction of any practical importance. Harold Reilly suggested, on page 73 of *The Edgar Cayce Handbook for Health* that maybe Cayce "was pre-cognitively aware that in the future there would be a new importance attached to the presence of zinc in the diet and sugar beets are high in zinc."

This may be true; I wouldn't care to argue the point. But it puzzles me none the less why he was so precise and explicit in regards to other precognitive matters that he shouldn't be precise and explicit in this one. Forty, fifty, sixty years ago sugar was not as pervasive in our diet as it is now. In the last fifty years sugar consumption has increased, according to informed estimates, from about 20 pounds per person per year to as much as 120 pounds per person per year in the United States. It is present not only in such obvious indulgences as ice cream, cookies, cake, and soda pop, but also in many hidden uses of sugar as in tomato sauce, catsup, mayonnaise, canned vegetables, bread, and many other staple but processed foods. One cannot help but wonder if Cayce was precognitive of zinc, why he was not precognitive about this truly alarming increase in sugar consumption.

Another example of what Cayce did not say has to do with water. Cayce recommended drinking eight glasses of water a day. It is not a particularly original or esoteric recommendation; many other health authorities suggest the same. But the point is that—to use two General Semantics techniques of thinking known as indexing and dating—water$_1$ is not the same as water$_2$—or, in ordinary language, water from a fresh mountain stream is not the same as water in New York City—and water$_{1940}$ is not the same as water$_{1984}$. In other words, the character of water differs drastically from one sample to another (as from place to another) and from one time frame to another. It may, in theory, still be healthful to drink eight glasses of water a day; but, in practice, considering the horrifying extent of water pollution, it could in many instances be downright dangerous to do so.

It should of course be noted that Cayce must have been aware of the dangers of bad water, because he sometimes told people not to drink the water in their area without boiling it, or else to drink spring water. So he certainly was not naive as regards differentiating between one source of water and another. The problem arises, however, when readers of the Cayce material are unaware of the differentiation he sometimes made, and unaware of the general danger of much of our water these days because of pollution and the excessive chemical treatment of our water supplies. They are unaware of it, or indifferent to it, because many of them, feeling they have found the Ultimate Answers in Cayce, limit their reading on diet and health to the Cayce readings and feel themselves safe in practicing his ideas without reading anything new.

Still another item which needs scrutiny is Cayce's frequent recommendation that people avoid red meats, ham, and rare steaks and roasts, and eat lamb, fish, and fowl instead. His prohibition of red meats especially has been vindicated by numerous recent

31

medical studies. I cannot say the same regarding lamb and fowl, but there are other very cogent reasons for not eating them whether orthodox medicine says anything about it or not. I refer to the current confinement methods of meat productions—not so much as regards lamb, perhaps—(the treatment of calves for veal is an abomination, however) but very distinctly as regards chickens.

The confinement of four and five chickens in one small wire-bottomed cage, with no exercise, sunshine, or fresh air is standard practice in most poultry "farms" today—resulting in both physical and psychological stress to the chickens. They are kept alive on antibiotics, tranquilizers, hormones, and all sorts of chemicals in their feed which logic tells us must leave a residue and have an effect on the quality of the meat and eggs so produced.

There are two considerations, then: (1) The eating of meat produced in this way may be highly dangerous to human beings—not in the sense of causing immediate death, but rather in the sense of the gradual accumulation of questionable toxins in the human system, many of them known to be carcinogenic. (2) There is a serious ethical issue involved: What right do we have to subject other living creatures to life-long immobility and frustration, just to serve our own appetites or our greed for profit?

Cayce constantly talked about "the Master"—meaning Jesus—and spoke of how we must imitate Him and demonstrate the fruits of the spirit: loving-kindness, mercy, compassion, gentleness, etc. Are these qualities supposed to stop with our own species, and not be expressed toward other forms of life? Would Cayce believe that Jesus—who said "As ye do it unto the least of these creatures ye do it unto me"—could walk indifferently by the wooden crates where calves with gentle, wondering eyes are kept from a few days after birth to slaughtering time—in total darkness (so the meat will be whiter) and in crates so small they cannot move (so the meat doesn't develop undesirable muscle)? If Cayce believed this, then I think I would lose much of my respect, great as it is, for Cayce.

But I do not think that Cayce, whether in his waking or in his super-conscious state, would be so insensitive. I believe that, as with water, sugar, coffee, and cigarettes, his statements reflect the safer, simpler conditions of his time; they do not reflect the sophisticated, dangerous, and, in the case of meat, cruel conditions of the present time.

It must be remembered that Cayce almost always was giving a reading to an individual who had a uniquely personal problem for which he gave a uniquely personal prescription. In some instances—

in fact, many—the prescription could be, and has been, safely generalized to other persons with a similar problem, even across a long span of time. But why should we expect Cayce to have said something like this: "Drink eight glasses of water a day. Of course, sixty years from now, I might qualify that"—any more than we would expect an ordinary physician to speak in the same vein? It is folly to expect total knowledge and total precognition from any psychic, no matter how excellent. And he was, indeed, an excellent psychic.

He has changed the lives, constructively and dramatically, of thousands of people. He has made them aware of their responsibility to discipline and change themselves, mentally, physically, and spiritually. He has given a sense of meaning and purpose to life in an epoch where chaos prevails and values have crumbled. He has provided an extraordinary confirmation of the validity of the clairvoyant faculty. He has been a great door-opener to what can be hoped will be a more illumined future. The Association for Research and Enlightenment which since 1933 has fostered the preservation, study, and dissemination of his material in the face of enormous difficulties, has steadfastly remained an honest and faithful custodian of this very important heritage.

I can only hope that its thousands of followers do not take the attitude ascribed to the Muslim caliph Omar who, when a certain philosopher asked to be given the great Alexandrian library, replied that if the thousands of books in the library agreed with the Koran they were unnecessary, and if they did not agree with it, they were false. Therefore they should all be destroyed. So the books of that great library of the ancient world were distributed to the public baths of Alexandria where for six months they served to feed the fires that heated the bath waters.

The story may be apocryphal, but the attitude it describes is not uncommon, and the moral it points to is very clear. To cling rigidly to one body of information, however inspired and inspiring, however important and however valid, to take cognizance only of what re-enforces that body of material, and to ignore everything else and especially everything else that is new, is not very wise.

The followers of the Cayce information as well as those of other psychically based groups would do well, I think, to take to heart three statements: one, made by Andrew Jackson Davis, a clairvoyant of the nineteenth century who did work very similar to that done by Edgar Cayce. "We are necessarily limited to the

*Reading 282-4.

33

sphere of our clairvoyant perception, aided by observation and the conclusions of reason. Consequently it is not supposable *that our answer to any question is a finality,* but a stepping stone rather to analyzation and conclusions far more profound and satisfactory." (italics mine)

Another pertinent statement, made by Edgar Cayce himself, is "Truth is a *growing* thing!" (282-4); and William R. Inge said many years ago: "There is no greater disloyalty to the great pioneers of human progress than to refuse to budge an inch from where they stood."

MISSIE: THE PSYCHIC DOG OF DENVER

Psychic magazine published this article in their October issue of 1973. I expressed the hope, in the final sentence, that the book which Mildred Probert was writing about Missie would give us more clues as to her little dog's extraordinary talent. Unfortunately Miss Probert died a few years ago, leaving an uncompleted manuscript about Missie which deserves to be completed and published.

Miss Probert once told me that at a conference in San Diego, after the death of Missie, a psychic told her that the very gifted child she should have had was still hovering around her and that this child had expressed herself through Missie. (It seems that Miss Probert had been engaged to be married but her fiance had died tragically before the wedding could take place.) I find this somewhat difficult to believe, even though, according to Miss Probert, other information the psychic gave her was highly evidential and the psychic was a total stranger to her and her phenomenal dog. And yet it is a strange universe we live in, filled with many strange things. And if one can accept the possibility of communication between the "here-living" and the "there-living" (as Pelley used to put it), why not through the instrumentality of a little dog? Probably not a common occurrence, but maybe a possible one.

People generally don't seem to believe me when I start to talk about the clairvoyant dog of Denver. "Oh?" they say, with an uncomplimentary inflection. "Did you ever see it perform?"

"No," I have to admit, "but I've met people who have. I've also seen at least a dozen notarized affadavits from prominent citizens and a number of newpaper articles about it."

This usually makes them a little more inclined to listen, and I then proceed to tell them the whole fascinating story.

I first heard of My Wee Missie, or, more simply, Missie, the psychic Boston terrier, when I was in Denver for a conference in 1967. I phoned the dog's owner, Miss Mildred Probert, and had a long conversation with her.

My impression of her over the phone was that she was a very well-informed and perfectly rational woman—an impression which was more than confirmed some months later when I met her in person at her home. In addition, I later found, she is an attractive lady and a very talented person artistically as well.

For reasons of health Miss Probert retired a few years ago from her profession of floral designer. At one time in her life she ran a pet store for a period of five years. After her retirement she took in birds and Boston terriers (her favorite breed) when they needed post-operative care, or when their owners were away on vacation. Missie had been brought to her because it was too tiny a puppy to nurse on its mother, and needed to be fed with an eye-dropper for some time after birth. The little dog never had a dog mother to train it, or dog brothers and sisters to orient it to normal dog life. This may or may not have been a significant factor in its future development. Another curious factor: the dog had dark blue eyes. I am told that the only blue eyes ever to be found in any canine breed are a very pale greenish blue.

Miss Probert told me that the little dog was close to five years old when she discovered that there was something unusual about it.

One day when she and her mother were walking the little dog outside their home, a young woman passed by with her small son in a baby stroller. They chatted a few moments, and then Miss Probert asked the child how old he was. The child didn't answer. The mother said that the child didn't talk very well yet, but that he was three years old. "Three. *Three. Three!*" said Miss Probert to the child. "Can't you say three?" The child remained silent, but Missie suddenly barked three times, very distinctly.

They all laughed, remarking on what a coincidence it was. In the spirit of fun, Miss Probert then turned to the dog and said, "Can you tell us your own age, Missie?" Without hesitation the dog barked four times—which was correct. "How old will you be next week?" Mildred pursued, remembering that the dog's birthday was just one week away. The dog barked five times.

Miss Probert knew nothing about the laws of probability or chance; but it struck her that these answers could hardly be coincidental. From then on she began asking the dog questions that could be answered numerically—such as "How many fingers am I holding up?" "How much are two and two? three and five?"—or with yes and no answers—three barks signifying yes, two barks signifying no. Invariably she got correct answers.

"What are the numbers of our street address?" was one of the early questions she asked. They lived at 4105 Stuart Street. The dog barked four times, paused, barked once, paused, sneezed, for the zero, and then barked five times.

"How many letters are there in my first name?" The dog barked seven times. "In my last name?" Another seven barks. Mildred Probert does indeed total seven and seven.

At this point in the story, listeners sometimes suspect that Miss Probert is giving the dog mental commands and that the dog is merely telepathic—"merely" being a curious put-down since telepathy itself would be no small feat.

However, according to her own testimony at least, Miss Probert never gave the dog mental commands. There is of course no direct way of proving this; but we do have considerable indirect evidence that she did not, for the dog replied, accurately, to anyone who questioned her—and did so on different occasions in five different languages—even when Miss Probert was absent from the room.

At a party one evening, the host held out a coin purse and asked Missie: "How many coins are in this purse?" Missie barked sixteen times. The man opened his purse and counted out sixteen pennies—an amount unknown to him and to everybody else.

Taking a deck of ordinary playing cards, another person asked the dog to bark out the number of spots on each card as he held it up. He held the cards in such a way that the back of the cards faced the dog and the assembled company, and at arm's length from himself so that he himself did not see the face of the card either. This was the first time Missie had ever seen a deck of playing cards, and yet she went through the entire deck without a mistake. Since nobody in the room saw the face of the cards until after Missie barked the response, at which time the experimenter showed the card to everyone, this would seem to preclude the possibility of telepathy and make it a clear-cut case of clairvoyance. (When she came to a Jack, Queen, or King, she whined: then she was asked "Is this a picture card?" She barked three times for yes. "Is it a King? Queen? Jack?" She would bark yes when he came to the corrct one.)

All told, in the course of her six-year career, Missie passed more than thirty-five kinds of psychic tests.

She answered correctly such questions as: What time is it?

What is the temperature? What is the date today? What is your veterinarian's phone number? What is this person's zip code?

Passing strangers sometimes became involved with conversations with Mildred apropos of the dog. In one such case Miss Probert asked Missie: "How many letters are there in this lady's first name?" Missie barked four times. Mildred asked the lady what her name was; it was Mary. "How many letters are there in *merry,* like Merry Christmas?" The dog barked five times. "In *marry,* like to get married?" The dog again barked five times. This experience led Mildred to ask the dog how many letters there were in such English words as *lamb, knight, knee, knife, knit,* etc.— words in which there were silent letters. Invariably the dog gave the right number of letters. Missie could also tell correctly the birthdate of anyone, whether an acquaintance or a total stranger, though Mildred told her to be discreet when it came to the birth year of ladies. The little dog would bark out the month and the day and then hang her head in silence as regards the year!

Missie's first psychic prediction was made on October 15, 1964. At that time everybody was interested in the outcome of the 1964 presidential election. Miss Probert had walked into a neighborhood furniture store, with Missie in her arms, as usual. The store personnel always enjoyed seeing Missie and asking her questions. Mildred said to the owner of the store: "How many weeks before election?" Before the man could answer, Missie barked three times which was correct. Somewhat surprised Mildred said, "How many days till election day, Missie?" The dog barked nineteen times which, on checking the calendar, proved to be exactly right.

The owner of the store said, "Ask her who will win!" "But how would she know that?" Mildred objected. Everyone standing around insisted. "Ask her!" So Mildred said: "If Mr. Johnson is one and Senator Goldwater is two, who will win the election?" Missie answered with one firm bark. Mildred then reversed the question: "If Barry Goldwater is one and Johnson is two, who will win?" Missie replied with two strong barks.

One of the bystanders thought that this was a newsworthy item and phoned the *Rocky Mountain News,* which promptly sent out a photographer and a reporter. On November 8, 1964, there appeared in that paper a picture of Missie together with her prediction. It was the first time she had predicted a future event of public interest. Later predictions included the outcome of other elections, of court cases, and of the correct number of delays on the launching of Gemini 12.

On New Year's Eve (the last day of the year 1965), she was

interviewed on Denver radio station KTLN—a program generally heard by about 90,000 people. The radio moderator asked her how many letters there were in Happy New Year; she barked them out correctly. What year are we in? She answered correctly. When will the New York transit strike end? She barked out January 13—which turned out to be corect. She was also asked about the very peculiar earthquake which had recently occurred in Denver. Was it due to natural causes? No, she said. When will we find out what caused it? In June, she replied. The following June it was discovered that the army had been putting waste material from nerve gases into an old well, and that this had caused the explosions which seemed like earthquake shocks.

The following day, New Year's Day, 1966, she predicted on another radio show who would win the World Series baseball games—the Dodgers—what day the series would end—a Wednesday—and what the score would be—six to nothing. Nine months later she was proven to be exactly right.

There are many cases on record in which Missie correctly predicted the sex of an unborn child, its date of birth, and its weight. One of the most astonishing of these cases is the following. On September 10, 1965, a very pregnant lady stopped to talk to Missie and Miss Probert as they sat on their front lawn. Mildred told her about the dog's gift for telling correct data about an unborn child. "Well," said the stranger, "I know all about mine. I lost two babies and I have an appointment with my doctor for a Caesarean on October 6."

"Will this lady have her baby on October 6?" Mildred asked Missie. Missie barked twice, for no. The woman began to cry, saying that this must mean that the baby would die like the others. Mildred immediately asked the dog if the baby would be alive. "Yes," she barked, three times.

"What month will the baby come?" Mildred asked.

"I already *know* that," objected the lady. "October!"

"No," barked the dog. She then turned to Mildred and gave nine barks, meaning September, and then two barks, pause, and eight barks, the 28th.

"A girl?" said Mildred. "No," barked the dog.

"A boy?" "Yes."

"That can't be right," said the lady, indignantly. "The doctor is positive that it will be a girl."

"At what time will the baby be born?"

The dog barked nine times.

"Nine o'clock in the morning?" "No."

"In the evening?" "Yes."

"Oh, that's impossible," objected the lady. "The doctor isn't in the clinic at 9 P.M. The Caesarian is scheduled for 9 A.M."

"How much will the baby weigh?" Seven, barked the dog.

"Well, I doubt that," said the lady. "My other babies were a puny five pounds."

She then took her leave, saying that she appreciated the dog's amazing comprehension of the questions, but that she was wrong on all the facts. Miss Probert requested that she telephone her when the baby was born.

Late the night of September 28 Miss Probert received an excited phone call from the lady's husband. "My wife became very sick this evening and had to be rushed to the hospital," he explained. "Her own doctor was out of town and she gave birth to a baby boy, naturally, at 9 P.M.!" "How much did it weigh?" asked Mildred. "Seven pounds!" exclaimed the proud father. "She's fine, he's fine, and we wanted you to know!"

Missie's fame slowly spread through radio and TV interviews and newspaper articles that appeared from time to time. Professors, doctors, lawyers, teachers, and other professional people came to see her. One very skeptical psychiatrist lost his skepticism when the dog correctly barked out the numbers of his social security number—which he himself had forgotten and had to look up to check.

Among the many notarized affadavits in Miss Probert's possession are some from radio moderators, superintendents of schools, veterinarians, and governmental officials. Here are a few samples:

November 13, 1967

In February 1965 we visited our neighbor Mildred Probert. She had her little clairvoyant Boston Terrier, My Wee Missie, answer some questions for us. She barked out the birth dates of our three daughters very plainly and easily understood. Missie also gave the number of letters in our names and the time of day and her own address, including the Zip code number.

Then my husband put the dog in a chair, leaned over her, and asked, "How many *months* will I live?" Miss Probert protested. She did not want her dog to predict death, and cautioned little Missie *not* to answer that question.

My husband insisted on the dog answering and would not release her. (He said he felt he would live only a few months— not years.) Missie answered his questions with "25." Miss

Probert quickly said, "Perhaps she means twenty-five *years.*"

He then asked the dog, "How many *years* will I live?" Missie answered immediately "2." He continued, "Could you tell me the date, the month?" Missie answered "4." He asked, "the day?" She replied "3." "1-9-6-7."

This event came true, *exactly* as the dog predicted. My husband, C. Kincaid, died on April 3, 1967. The fourth month, third day, twenty-five months (two years), later. All the members of our family saw Missie perform her gift of prophesying innumerable times.

Norma Kincaid Price

To Whom It May Concern:

When I was moderator on a radio talk show on station K.T.L.N. Denver, Colo. I had a phone call from Mildred Probert on 9/30/65 (the day my baby girl was born.) Miss Probert told me her "psychic dog," a Boston terrier, had been barking out a "yes" answer, when asked if my baby would be a girl.

This call was made before the baby was born.

She put the dog on the phone to bark out the hour of time it was then and the temperature, which I checked with a phone temperature call.

Missie also gave the date, Miss Probert asking "what month, date, year, and the day of the week?" And how many letters in my name? All without error. It brought a rush of calls when I remarked it was "the first time I talked to a dog and it answered back!"

After that Missie performed over the phone on my program seven or eight times giving scores for forthcoming football games and the World Series baseball games, correctly.

On New Year's Eve 1966, she gave answers for events occurring each month for that next year. All turned out to be true.

Gary Robertson

To Whom It May Concern:

One day in the spring of 1966, while visiting Miss Mildred Probert, her little Boston Terrier, named My Wee Missie, gave quite a performance for me.

To my amazement the little dog, when asked by Miss Probert, barked out correctly my social security number, my phone number and address and the number of letters in the street on which I live. She then gave the complete birth date;

month and year.

She responded without hesitation and Miss Probert gave her no cues of any sort. Miss Probert would not have known these numbered items mentioned above. I can only respond to all this in much the same way someone in Shakespeare's play, *Hamlet,* Act 1, Scene V, says to Horatio, "There are more things in heaven and earth, Horatio, than are dreamt of in your philosophy."

Respectfully submitted,

Dennis Gallagher,
House of Representatives,
The State of Colorado,
Denver.

It was a sad day for Miss Probert when little Missie died. After age six, the little dog had been subject to epileptic attacks; but death came from choking on some candy she had eaten on May 21, 1966, three days prior to her eleventh birthday.

What can account for the strange phenomenon of Missie? Was Missie a medium, controlled by some human spirit? Was Missie a superdog? We may never know, though the full story to be told in a book being written by Miss Probert may give us further clues to the enigma of Missie.

THE SOUL-SEARCHING TRIAL IN PHOENIX

I was living in Los Altos, California, at the time I wrote this article. The story of James Kidd, the old Arizona prospector who left a quarter of a million dollars to anyone who could prove the existence of the soul, captured my imagination, as it did the imagination of thousands of others.

I personally had no way of proving the soul's existence, but I was curious as to how the many claimants to the fortune would attempt to do so. So, much as I dislike hot weather, I made a special trip to Phoenix in June 1967 to attend the hearings, which proved to be truly bizarre.

The judge's decision to award the fortune to the Barrows Neurological Institute—after court sessions lasting three months and one week and costing the Arizona taxpayers an inordinate amount of money—was, I felt, preposterous. The decision was appealed, and rightfully so. The Supreme Court of Arizona did not schedule a hearing until almost four years later, at which time the judge's decision was overturned. The money was finally awarded to an appropriate recipient: the American Society for Psychical Research in New York City.

Psychic magazine published my account of this case in their July/ August 1971 issue.

I gnorance of the law is no excuse," many a judge has said from the bench. But some peculiar things happen when the ignorance is on the judge's side of the bench and the "laws" are those of psychic phenomena.

A dramatic case in point is the 1967 trial in a Phoenix, Arizona, courtroom, popularly known as the Soul-Searching Trial or the Great Soul Trial. John G. Fuller used the latter term as the title of his conscientious and sensitive book on the subject, *The Great Soul Trial* (Macmillan, 1970). The trial was concerned with executing the will of an Arizona miner, who left all of his considerable fortune to anyone who would "research" or "provide some scientific proof of the soul of the human body which leaves at death."

The hearing lasted three months and one week—probably the longest and the most expensive in the history of Arizona. Judge Robert L. Myers listened to the appeals of some 133 individuals and organizations who felt they deserved the money. Finally, after "receiving divine guidance," he said, he awarded the money to the Barrows Neurological Institute of Phoenix, a half-million dollar endowed institute which does research, principally with cats and dogs, on the brain and central nervous system.

Whatever divinity was guiding Judge Myers in his decision apparently was not paying close attention when the four scientists who represented the Barrows Neurological Institute stated in court that they did not believe that any part of the human being survives the body, that they were not at that time doing any research into such a possibility, and that they would probably not in the future do any such research, even if they got the money. One of the scientists was, in fact, he said, "embarrassed" by the very word "soul."

It was the opinion of some persons that the judge's decision was a local or politically expedient one, in that he awarded it to a local institution. This may or may not be true. But it seemed to parapsychologically informed people that the judge's decision was not in accord with the intent of Kidd's will, and that it was, in fact, a serious miscarriage of justice.

Four of the petitioners felt this so strongly that they appealed the decision. These were two organizations: The American Society for Psychical Research (ASPR) of New York and the Psychical Research Foundation (PRF), of Durham, N.C. and two individuals: Reverend Russell Dilts of Indiana, and Dr. Joseph Still of El Monte, California.

It took three years after the appeals were made for the Arizona Supreme Court to get around to the matter, and finally, almost four years later, this February, the Arizona Supreme Court reversed Judge Myers's decision. Chief Justice Fred Stuckmeyer— an Episcopalian who (according to the report in *Newsweek* for February 8, 1971) is not impressed with scientific materialism as a substitute for the Christian view of the world—ruled that to study the central nervous system was not what Kidd had in mind. He instructed the lower court to withhold the funds from Barrows, and to award them instead to one or more of the four who appealed the decision.

The Barrows Neurological Institute, understandably miffed, promptly demanded a rehearing. The rehearing was denied, and Barrows will have to struggle along as best it may with its grants from the United States Department of Health, the National Science Foundation, the United States Navy, and other relatively affluent sources for vivisectional and other physiological research of the central nervous system.

James Kidd, the old miner who made the will, may be looking on from other dimensions and feeling much happier than he has been for the past four years. (As a matter of fact, in a seance held with English medium Douglas Johnson shortly after the judge's decision, author John Fuller was told that some one was present, a very old man, whose name began with K. "He says," reported Johnson, "'I don't think much of the result. . . .It's probably been a waste of money.'" "He's chuckling," added Johnson. "It's something about a Pandora's box.")

The personality of Kidd is something of an enigma. He lived frugally, in a $4 a week room, and almost like a recluse. He smoked nickel cigars and was known to have the habit of picking up discarded newspapers in the restaurant where he often ate. He worked for some years as a pumpman in an Arizona copper mine. An injury caused him to retire from his regular job, and he became an independent prospector, working his own claims. Unknown to his few friends, he had through the years invested his modest earnings in stocks. It was not unusual for him to disappear for several days at a time; but in November of 1949 at the age of sixty-seven (or, perhaps, seventy), he disappeared never to return again.

In May of 1958 the E. F. Hutton Company, an investment firm, reported to the Arizona state tax commissioner that dividends to Kidd had not been acknowledged or cashed for a number of years. Mrs. Swift, the state tax commissioner, opened Kidd's safety deposit box and found stock certificates worth about $100,000. She also found stock buying slips, a few photographs of Kidd, and other miscellaneous items; and, on the second or third examination of the box's contents, a small hand-scribbled will, unseen on first examination because it was tucked away with a packet of stock buying slips. The will read as follows:

> This is my first and only will and is dated the 2nd day in January, 1946. I have no heirs, have not been married in my life, and after all my funeral expenses have been paid and $100 to some preacher of the gospitel (sic) to say farewell at my grave, sell all my property which is all in cash and stock with

E. F. Hutton Co., Phoenix, some in safety box, and have this balance money to go in a research or some scientific proof of a soul of the human body which leaves at death. I think in time there can be a photograph of the soul leaving the human at death. James Kidd.

Some of the members of the staff in the Attorney General's office felt that the will was obviously a joke. It is not on record whether any of them said, "He's got to be Kidding"; but judging from the frequency with which journalists subsequently felt impelled to say things in this vein, someone probably did. These same staff members also felt that the will should be quietly destroyed and the money simply put into the state's general fund. But Mrs. Swift believed that the will should be honored and submitted to the courts, and she acted upon this conviction.

In 1962 Kidd was declared legally dead, all efforts to trace him having failed. In 1964 the will was admitted to probate. The matter had been written up in the press, and long before the trial actually began, much interest had been generated. This is not surprising, in view of the fact that when the assets of Kidd's estate had been more thoroughly investigated, and the dividends and accumulated interest included, it was found that its value was close to $225,000, or roughly a quarter of a million dollars.

By March 17 of 1967, more than 4,500 pieces of mail had been received by the court, from people who felt they could prove the existence of the soul and were therefore entitled to the fortune. Almost every country of the world was represented, with the exception of Ireland; eighty-seven letters came from India alone; forty-seven from Germany, twenty-one from Canada; twenty from South America, and sixteen from France. Judge Myers, whose hobby is stamp collecting, said there was one good thing about the foreign correspondence: he would get to keep all the stamps.

Many of the letters were illiterate. A high percentage of the persons who wrote argued that the proof of the soul was to be found in the Bible. Some people said they would be happy to prove the existence of the soul if the court would pay their traveling expenses. A woman in Canada wrote: "I wouldn't be human if I didn't wish for some of Kidd's loot to buy me a new set of teeth." A man in Brazil said: "The human body has two souls, a white soul and a black soul. Which one do you want me to prove the existence of?" Somebody who claimed to be St. Mark and Wagner phoned Judge Myers's office and said he wanted to talk about the soul, which he proceeded to do to Judge Myers's clerk for fifteen minutes. This was just a small sampling—in terms of virtual illiteracy, thinly veiled self-interest, and strange psychically slanted opinions—of what was yet to come.

Most of those who wrote to the court were not able to travel to Phoenix and pay the $15 filing charge. But at least 133 claimants—most of them sincere, most of them truly convinced of the importance of what they had to say, and many of them with some very valid extrasensory evidences—did appear. They provided the Superior Court of Maricopa County with what surely must have been one of the strangest and most colorful court cases in the history of Arizona.

It began the morning of June 6, 1967, in the mercifully air-conditioned courtroom of the Superior Court. The room, modern and walnut-paneled, comfortably seats about eighty people, though in the early days of the trial more crowded in. Presiding Judge Myers, an Episcopalian (rather than a Mormon or Catholic, like so many in Phoenix), at one time served in the state legislature. He is a man known for his thoroughness, his fairness, and his integrity. Faced with an unusual and unprecedented case, he conducted the court with dignity, courtesy, and patience throughout.

However, it was apparent from the outset that he knew practically nothing of the extensive data relating to the survival problem, so carefully accumulated by psychical researchers over the past 100 years. Like many other professional persons who are the products of a narrow compartmentalization in professional education, the judge's ignorance was not surprising.

But Judge Myers's ignorance of psychic matters obviously affected both his procedures in the courtroom and his final decision. In early July, after the trial had been in process for several weeks, he was quoted by the *Phoenix Gazette* as saying that too many persons "believe the trial to be an 'essay contest,' and the one who can give the most convincing arguments that there is a soul will get the money." This naivete on the part of many persons is understandable, the state of parapsychological education being what it is, but the judge would not have been confronted with this situation if the court procedures he set up had been more well-advised in the first place.

There was, for example, a Lt. Col. Virat Ambudha who, at an expense of $4,000 to himself, came all the way from Bangkok, Thailand, to present his case or as he put it, to "claim his reward" for having already proved the existence of the soul. His hope, if he won Kidd's fortune, was to print in all languages and distribute throughout the world a book called "Increasing Brain Power" which he had written concerning the soul, and thus "transform this passionate human world" into "a paradise world" and bring about world peace. In his careful but hard to understand English he quoted extensively from his book. A sample of his reasoning: "An engine cannot go without an engineer; and a body cannot function without a soul. So when the body dies the soul must go on." Questionable logic, and hardly proof in the modern sense of the term.

In the same general category of logical argument would fall the case of a thirty-nine-year-old Catholic professor of psychology and philosophy Richard Carl Spurney, of Mt. San Antonio College, California. Spurney compared the human brain to an unopened can of spaghetti: long strips of white stuff (neuron chains) in a red sauce (blood). He went on to say that physical substance alone, whether spaghetti or a human brain, is incapable of thought and feeling. Hence thought and feeling indicate the presence of something non-material in man. Professor Spurney dramatized his idea of the separate identities of the brain and the mind (which, he said, could be equated roughly with the soul) with some visual aids: a can of spaghetti, a TV set, three grapefruit, and three apples. His line of reasoning was interesting, but it was hardly to be called scientific proof.

Also in the catagory of the philosophical and the speculative was the petition of the Northern Arizona State College Department of Philosophy. Five philosophy instructors proposed to set up a James Kidd Chair of Philosophy at their college, the purpose of which was to define the soul through philosophical, literary, and religious study. How could you tell if you had discovered the soul, they said, if you did not first know what the soul *was?* This sounds logical enough; but on the other hand we cannot help but think how fortunate we all are that Edison did not wait to find out exactly what electricity *was* before he worked out a method of using it. If he had set up a Chair of Philosophy to study the matter with scholastic methods of definition, we might still be using candles in the year 3000.

All of the time and money wasted in hearing the petitions of this type could have been saved by the simple expedient of disqualifying them at the very outset. An examining committee— selected from professional persons thoroughly familiar with the data of psychical research, which includes the problem of scientific proof—should have been set up, with the authority of screening from the courtroom the many petitioners who could not possibly provide the kind of scientific research or proof that Kidd obviously had in mind.

As it was, any claimant could present his case in court by merely paying the $15 fee and filing a written claim with the clerk of the Superior Court. This procedure opened the door not only to those who had nothing to offer but logical arguments, but also to many who were tranparently mercenary, illiterate, or unequipped to deal with the technical problems involved.

There was another category of applicants, namely those who had had some kind of psychic experience. Among these was Bishop Robert Raleigh of the Church of Antioch, Thousand Oaks, California.

The Bishop had gone blind after an automobile accident. Doctors told him he would never see again. "But a holy being appeared to me in the inner planes," he testified, "and told me that I would have a healing from my blindness." The holy being also told him about the soul and other spiritual matters. His blindness was healed two weeks later.

A seventy-two-year-old man of Catholic background, Paul Mettie, also reported on various psychic experiences, as did a gentleman from California, Mr. Joe Surney, who claimed a miraculous recovery from apparent death at the age of one year. There were numerous others.

It is understandable that vivid personal experiences of this type would convince the recipient of them of the reality of the soul. Unfortunately, however, as the long history of psychical research has repeatedly shown, what's proof to the goose, so to speak, is not proof to the gander. In other words, what is overwhelmingly convincing to an individual may be unconvincing to an outsider who did not witness the event and can find no objective evidence of its reality. One is reminded of Thomas Paine's astute observation in *The Age of Reason* regarding religious revelation. "Admitting, for the sake of a case," he wrote, "that something has been revealed to a certain person, it is revelation to that person only. When he tells it to a second person, a second to a third, a third to a fourth, and so on, it ceases to be revelation to all those persons. It is revelation to the first person only, and *hearsay* to every other, and consequently they are not required to believe it."

Some petitioners, however, did recognize the need to submit objective evidence, and attempted to give a psychic demonstration in court. Among these was Mrs. Jean Bright, an Encino, California, housewife and mother, who claimed that she was in constant contact with a dentist friend of hers who died in 1965. Whenever she asks a question of him, she said, the soul of the departed dentist twitches the muscles of her head, face, or legs.

To show that she was not hearing the questions and answers, she put earplugs in her ears and sat under a noisy hairdryer. Then she answered, by spasmodic twitches of her head, twelve yes-and-no questions put to her by her mother, who was standing behind her.It is reported that she got eight answers out of twelve correct, concerning such minor matters as the color of Mrs. Bright's hair, the time of day, the temperature, etc. Perhaps there are good psychic reasons why the dentist missed such questions as "Did Barry Goldwater come from Arizona?" "No" and "Is today (Wednesday) Saturday?" "Yes"; but the demonstration apparently did not convince the judge.

The two individuals who appealed Judge Myers's decision were Rev. Russell Dilts, a Spiritualist medium from South Bend, Indiana, and Dr. Joseph W. Still, a medical doctor of El Monte, California, who was represented in the appeal, incidentally, by famous San Francisco attorney Melvin Belli.

Rev. Dilts produced some photographic exhibits purporting to be psychic pictures of James Kidd and various members of Kidd's family obtained after their death. Dr. Still rested his case on a theory of his regarding three levels of life and death which he defined as being organismal, psychic, and vegetative. Rev. Dilts was the only one (to this author's knowledge) who spoke directly to the suggestion made by Kidd in his will: "I think in time there can be a photograph of the soul leaving the human at death," and presented evidence in court pointing to that possibility.

However, there are many ways of producing "psychic" pictures fraudulently. While Dilts's photos may be completely authentic, no scientist would acknowledge them as "proof" of anything unless they had been produced under rigorous test conditions and were repeatable under the same kind of conditions. As for Dr. Still, the case he presented is interesting, but unproven in any strict sense. Besides, even it if could be shown that there are three stages in dying, it does not establish that anything survives permanently thereafter.

Perhaps the wisest disposition of Kidd's money (which now, incidentally, amounts to about $300,000, due to the securities being sold at the height of the market and the sum being put in savings and loan companies) would seem to be, not to any single individual, but some well-qualified organization which is in a position to pursue soul research in a professional manner.

The two psychical research organizations which appealed Myers's decision, and which were named by the Supreme Court decision as proper possible recipients of the money, were the

American Society for Psychical Research, with headquarters in New York City, and the Psychical Research Foundation based, under the direction of W. G. Roll, in Durham, North Carolina.

The ASPR is, of course, the oldest organization of its kind in the country, and has to its credit such distinguished members as psychologist William James. Since 1886, it has been doing careful studies into all aspects of psychical research, including the survival problem.

The Psychical Research Foundation, created in 1960 with an endowment from Charles Ozanne, has from the outset taken as its prime objective the scientific study of survival. Both organizations presented solid, serious cases; both have impressive records of achievement; and either one of them or both would undoubtedly use the Kidd money to its best advantage.

It is particularly interesting, in the light of recent breakthroughs, that Kidd said: "I think in time there can be a photograph of the soul leaving the human at death." Though he was, by all reports, an uneducated man, and though his will was clumsily expressed, none the less he had here a very valid intuition. (It is not known whether or not Kidd knew of the photographic experiments of the nineteenth-century French researcher Baraduc, who claimed to have photographed the soul of his wife leaving the body at death.)

The Ted Serios phenomenon (*The World of Ted Serios,* Jule Eisenbud, 1967), while not pointing directly to survival, none the less shows that photography holds important scientific possibilities in psychical research. The Kirlian photographic process—developed in Russia by a man and wife and reported on in *Psychic Discoveries Behind the Iron Curtain* (Ostrander and Schroeder, 1970) and "Psychic Enigmas and Energies in the U.S.S.R." (*Psychic,* May/June 1971) seemingly makes it possibly to photograph a secondary body (called the bio-plasmic body by the Russians but probably the equivalent of the "astral" or "etheric" body). Who knows but what some future refinement of the Kirlian process could lead to photographic evidence of something leaving the body at death. How long this "something" might survive after death is a question closely linked with the study of the enigma of human consciousness.

What the final outcome of the Kidd case will be is not know at the time of this writing. But whatever the outcome, at least two morals can be drawn from this story. The first is: there is an urgent need for the dissemination of psychic information at academic, scientific, and legal levels. The second: where there is a will, there is a way: a way to misinterpret and circumvent it, unless it is made highly specific, and without loopholes. Let all will-makers take heed.

PART II: A NEW APPROACH TO WISDOM: GENERAL SEMANTICS

When I lived in Santa Barbara (my favorite town in the whole world) I taught a class in General Semantics in Adult Education. I was acquainted at the time with a woman who was raising her very precocious five-year-old grandson. His name was Randolph. Randolph couldn't pronounce his R's very well; he referred to himself as Wandolph. Yet he picked up an amazing number of long words from his grandmother, who was something of an intellectual.

Sometimes, though, he got them confused. I remember one example of this especially.

He was riding in a car with his grandmother and several other women, and they happened to pass my house on Garden Street. "Oh, that's where Gina lives!" he exclaimed. "She's a fanatic!"

"Randolph!" said his grandmother. "Why do you say that?"

"You told me!" he returned. "She's a fanatic! She teaches General Fanatics!"

This was not the first time or the last that I have heard the word confused. Not long ago a grown woman told me she wondered when I would be giving another seminar in General Symmetrics; she wanted so much to take it.

I must admit, though, that there was just a kernel of truth in what Wandolph said. I *have* been something of a fanatic about General Semantics. At least I have had an unfailing devotion to its principles practically all of my adult life, and I have probably given close to 2,000 classes and lectures on the subject—to prisoners, to business executives in Tokyo, to aerospace engineers, to social workers, medical students, psychology students, church groups, adult education groups, etc., etc.

However, in self-defense let me say that I am not a fanatic in the sense that I talk about the subject interminably and indiscriminately to anyone I meet. In fact I rarely talk about it socially. Nor am I a fanatic in the sense that I think General Semantics can solve all the world's problems. I recognize that what General Semantics does in enabling people to think clearly and sanely, and therefore to improve their behavior patterns, is something no other system can do; but I also recognize that it doesn't do everything. I very clearly see its limitations.

Perhaps it is worth stating here that *to recognize a person's—or a system's—limitations is not equivalent to rejecting the person, or the system.* I have tried to make this point elsewhere, in my discussion of psychics in general ("On This Diet Eat Everything, Just Don't Swallow") and of Cayce in particular ("Edgar Cayce Revisited"). It is just as true of General Semantics as it is of anything else. Extract the good. Be aware of, but not unduly influenced by, the bad. Or, as Cayce use to put it: Maximize the virtues; minimize the faults. An old Colonial motto for wives is also apropos: "Be to his virtues very kind; be to his faults a little blind." And finally, a General Semantics idea, that of Non-Allness ("Nobody knows everything about anything") points to exactly the same healthy attitude.

For me at least the many merits of General Semantics outweigh its limitations.

The following articles deal with various aspects of my interest in the subject.

FABLE

While I was attending the University of Wisconsin, I had a friend with an antic sense of humor by the name of Paul Kroening III. We were introduced, briefly, by a mutual friend. For some reason which I don't recall we started writing to each other, and the friendship lasted, entirely by mail, for several years. Paul always wrote in a comic vein, and under many different aliases. One of the most frequent was Lesser—of Lesser and Boll Weevil, Attorneys at Law—or possibly it is only that the Lesser of Two Weevils remains especially in my memory. I remember also how on every December 24, without fail, I would receive a postcard (obviously from Paul) announcing the Annual Meeting at midnight of the Santaclaustrophobia Branch of the Scrooge Society, and signed, in a quavering hand, by Marley's Ghost.

It was Paul who first made me aware of the existence of something called semantics. I had neglected to write for him for almost a month, probably because of term papers or exams. One day I received a postcard from him reading: "What can have happend to Cerminara? Could she be taking a seminar in semantics in a cemetery?"

Never having seen the word 'semantics' before, I promptly looked it up in a dictionary. The definition was dull and forgettable, but a few weeks later another friend said he was reading a great book about semantics called Language in Action, *by Hayakawa. His enthusiasm reawakened my curiosity. I borrowed the book, which actually dealt with General Semantics, the system of thinking formulated by Alfred Korzybski, rather than just semantics, a branch of linguistics dealing with the changes in the meanings of words. I read the book with mounting excitement. It clarified many things for me, opened more intellectual doors than almost anything else I'd studied in college, and gave me a method with which to do my Ph.D. thesis—a case history study in improving personality through improving conversational skill. It also left me with an infatuation with the subject that has lasted ever since.*

On another occasion Paul wrote me a postcard saying, simply, "Did you know that there is no word in the English language that rhymes with lemon." *I accepted this poignant bit of information as a challenge, soon discovered a rhyme (of sorts) for* lemon, *and wrote the following poem incorporating it, which was later published in the university literary magazine. The poem reflects my distaste for college sorority teas, as well as my growing awareness, thanks to General Semantics, of how people who give you a choice of* either *this* or *that, are causing you—sometimes manipulatively—to think that there are no other possible alternatives. (In the case of tea, for example, why must it always be either cream or lemon? Why can't it be both? Or neither? Or almond extract? Or even rum? If rum does as much for tea as it does for cake and custard, it might be a great improvement.)*

FABLE

AWalrus of a gentle mien
Was standing by a soup tureen
⠀⠀⠀—and said

In manner sweetly feminine
"Will you have cream or lemon in
⠀⠀⠀—your soup?"

I firmly grasped my handkerchief
And stammered, "I'll take BOTH, ma'am, if
⠀⠀⠀—you please!"

She looked at me with unbelief
And answered: "Dear, I'd just as lief
⠀⠀⠀—but it

Is not ALLOWED, you know. The law
Would seem to be without a flaw
⠀⠀⠀—for no

One has complained so far, and who,
With all respect, my dear, are you
⠀⠀⠀—or I

That we should venture to defy
Thuswise Society's reli-
⠀⠀⠀—able

Dictates? Ah, no, 'tis safer far

To leave such things just as they are.
  —Would you

Like cream or lemon in your soup?

THE MORAL, friends, is not obscure.
If you would not appear a boor
  —you *must*

Take either cream OR lemon in your soup!

FAREWELL TO ELWOOD MURRAY

One summer I went to the University of Denver to attend the classes of Professor Elwood Murray. Professor Murray is well known in General Semantics circles as one of the early popularizers of the subject. Korzybski's rather formidable book, Science and Sanity, had appeared in 1933. Professor Murray at once saw its importance for education, and it was due to his influence as head of the department of English and Speech that the entire department was revamped a few years later so as to be based entirely on a General Semantics foundation.

Murray—now retired—was an innovative teacher. The class projects he assigned were intended to make students really use General Semantics principles rather than merely know them intellectually, to parrot back on examinations and then forget. In the summer session that I attended, he would devote the first hour of every three-hour class to a lecture on some General Semantics ideas. Then he would divide the class into three groups, and in the second hour, each group had to make preparations for a co-operative presentation during the third hour. One group had to go to the board and in a series of cartoon pictures illustrate some situation which would have been helped (or was helped) by the application of the principle Murray had just discussed. The second group had to create and present a short skit dramatizing the use (or lack of use) of the principle. And the third group had to find as many applications of the principle to practical life as possible, selecting the best ones for presentation in a talk by one member of the group to the class afterward.

These were mind-stretching exercises, and not always easy to do; but, thanks to Professor Murray's genial personality, a spirit of fun usually prevailed. Dubbing myself Poet Laureate of the class, I wrote the following poem at the end of the summer session, and the professor seemed to enjoy it.

AT THE END OF A SUMMER SESSION, FAREWELL TO ELWOOD MURRAY

Dear Professor Elwood Murray:
    After all the fun and fury
    The time has come for us
To say farewell.

We really hate to say it, and
We wish we could delay it;
But all good things
Get tolled their parting knell.

We came here egocentric,
Introverted and eccentric,
We leave in a much
Improved condition.*

We've lost a few rigidities
(Perhaps a few frigidities...)
To be flexible is now
Our chief ambition!

Thanks to you and to Non-Allness
We've outgrown some of our smallness.
We know that we will never
Be the same!

We live now by reality
And by extensionality.
That's why we'll have
More fun than Auntie Mame.

We've read Johnson's book and Lee's,
We have studied Ruesch and Kees,
We have also come to grips
With Hayakawa.

But Hayakawa's so abstruse
(Or is it just that we're obtuse?)

---

*Except for a few characters who are now more egocentric, introverted, and eccentric than before. Names on request.

Why don't you write
An easy *Lowa*kawa?

We confess: we used profanity
In reading (?) SCIENCE AND SANITY.
But then we learned
Semantic relaxation.

This method is, we find,
Very fine for peace of mind;
(Though we still prefer
Romantic relaxation.*)

We've gone through idiot antics
In the name of G. Semantics
And at times we've wished to
God we weren't here.

But when all is said and done
It's been really lots of fun
And (despite your crazy shirts)
You're quite a dear.

So if "heaven" does exist,
And St. Peter's got a list,
We know beyond a doubt
You've got it made.

We think you are The Best!
We have only one request.
Be sure to give us all
A passing grade.

---

*Non-verbal. A deux. See Ruesch and Kees, *Non-Verbal Communication*, p. 427½.

TOWARD SANITY ON THE PLANET

At the time that I was giving a class in General Semantics in Santa Barbara, California, I was invited to write a series of articles on the subject for a new magazine called The Santa Barbaran. *I accepted the invitation with enthusiasm, and wrote the piece which is here reprinted and which was to have been the first of the series. Unfortunately the magazine was short-lived, expiring after the first issue. This was the first time I had spoken in print about General Semantics, and in the article I suggested how its methods could do what religion does not always succeed in doing: bring about constructive psychological and social changes without the fanaticism and other aberrations that sometimes accompany religious persuasion.*

Fourteen years later, in a book entitled Insights For The Age of Aquarius, *I expanded on this theme, and in addition analyzed the basic semantic reasons for religious divisions and hatreds. The book has won a small but devoted following. Its title, perhaps, has been an obstacle to its being more widely known, since it suggests that it deals with astrology. In all probability anti-astrology people don't pick it up for that reason; and pro-astrology people pick it up, and seeing it has nothing to do with astrology, as quickly put it down. Its original subtitle in the Prentice-Hall hardback edition, was "A Scientific Analysis of the Problems of Religion"—a description which would frighten even me if I saw it on a bookstore counter. Fortunately I was able to persuade the editor of the Quest Books softcover edition to change the subtitle to "A Handbook for Religious Sanity," which is highly appropriate. When the book first came out someone told me at a literary party that he thought the book was called* Incest for Aged Aquarians. *That title would doubtless have sold many more copies.*

Bernard Shaw once remarked that this planet was probably the lunatic asylum of the solar system.

He could be right.

61

One Santa Barbaran I know (a fabulous character who, when he is not making terrible puns or studying ancient Pali texts, is dictating brilliant tape-recorded discourses on the psychology of self-integration) has a plan to found a place of refuge for those few inhabitants of earth who remain uninfected by the mental and moral degeneracies of our age. He calls it a Sane Asylum. All applicants for admission will be carefully screened.

Both Shaw and my friend are exaggerating, no doubt. And yet their exasperation at the spectacle of contemporary human idiocy is not unfounded. And it is shared by a goodly company of other thinkers and students who also diagnose our society as being basically unsane and sick. For more reasons than one we need to take stock of ourselves. We need to become more self-aware and then, desperately, we need to become more self-corrective.

Religion could certainly be an instrument for both these objectives. For many it has served this purpose and for many it continues to do so. But in the current crisis religion seems to have only a limited appeal, and therefore only a limited scope of effectiveness. Even outside the confines of atheistic Russia the prevailing temper of our age is skeptical, irreligious.

To make matters worse, religion, among those it *does* reach, is all too often itself the source of division and hostility. This is due not so much to the religion itself, in its essence, as to the rigidities of its adherents.

Prince Modupe, African-born dancer and musician who tells his life history in a fascinating new book called *I Was a Savage*— made a telling observation recently in a public lecture. He said that when his people lived in untouched isolation they lived harmoniously and with a sense of unity with each other and with God. When Christian missionaries of two different faiths appeared— one converting some of the tribesmen and the other converting others—all sorts of confusions and hatreds arose—matters not being helped by the pictures one of the missionaries brought showing all the angels in heaven as white-skinned and the devil and all his subjects as being black.

What happened in a remote African village is not of trivial significance—especially in a decade when churches may already be calling board meetings to discuss the crying need to prepare for missionary activities on the moon....If religionists disagree among themselves—not amicably, as they might, not acknowledging with humility the multi-faceted nature of truth and our own imperfect perception of it—but obstinately, with bigotry, spleen, and even fanatical hatred—and if they induce hostility among mankind rather than harmony and co-operative love—then surely there is something wrong.

Psychology, psychiatry, and sociology—those branches of science which are most directly concerned with human behavior—offer some promise. Yet sociologists are usually observers rather than changers of the social scene. And psychologists—though they offer insight and practical expedients—seem not to be equal, either numerically or in breadth of view—to solve our immediate planetary dilemma. And psychiatry, in a word, is expensive.

Since 1933 there has existed, however, a system of thinking which—though not itself a religion or a psychology—and though not in competition with either—does offer one way out of our problem, one inexpensive and almost universally available way into sanity. The system to which I refer is called General Semantics, and it is the creation of a Polish scientist called Alfred Korzybski.

It is necessary at this point to make something clear. General Semantics is *not* the same as semantics. It is *not* the study of words. And its business is *not* with defining your terms or establishing your referents.

Its concern, rather, is with the interaction of words and people. As one writer put it, General Semantics is about what people do to words—and what words do to people. It is, in a sense, a new kind of logic. It is also a technique, as Hayakawa puts it, of how not to be a damn fool.

Its name was, perhaps, an unfortunate choice on the part of Korzybski. When people are not confusing it with semantics (or even—believe it or not—with ceramics) they are shying away from it because it sounds so academically abstruse. Actually, it could just as well have been called General Evaluations—because evaluation is one of the basic things it is concerned with—but even this title might not have conveyed to the man in the street its immensely practical importance and its really unequalled effectiveness as a clarifier of thought and a saver of otherwise wasted emotional energy.

Perhaps I sound unfashionably, absurdly enthusiastic. I hope so. Because I am. My enthusiasm is shared by an increasing number of professional people all over the world—including psychiatrists, psychologists, writers, dentists, optometrists, doctors, parole officers, lawyers, educators, businessmen, and ministers, to name but a few. In forthcoming issues I shall endeavor to familiarize you with some of the detailed workings of General Semantics and how you can apply it to your daily living.

AN ANSWER TO A SOCIOLOGIST'S ATTACK ON GENERAL SEMANTICS

I admire the works of Pitirim Sorokin on many counts, and find his chapter on "The Five Dimensions of Love" in The Ways and Power of Love *especially original. To me, this material is more operationally useful and gives more insight into the cultivation of love than anything I have ever read elsewhere; and I have lectured about it many times.*

However, there is one aspect of Sorokin's work that I have not found admirable, and that is his repeated attacks on General Semantics.

As I have mentioned earlier (in the Introduction to Part II of this book) I am well aware of the fact that General Semantics has its limitations. And I feel that some of the criticisms that have been leveled against it are quite justifiable. Sorokin's, however, seemed to me to be totally unjustifiable, and gave evidence of a very superficial acquaintance with the subject.

The following article is the result of my concern, and it was published in ETC. *magazine (one of the two General Semantics publications) in December 1975.*

In San Jose, not long ago, a young man of my acquaintance was asked at a party what he had been doing with himself lately. He replied that he had been studying General Semantics. "What's that?" someone inquired. He launched into an explanation and a small group formed about him. "In my opinion, everybody ought to get into a GS session.* It has changed my life, and I think it would change most people's lives for the better." As he was saying this, a woman approached, carrying her cocktail glass, several drinks already to her credit.

"How dare you say such a thing!" she declared, loudly. "GS is decadent and immoral. This is what is causing our country to go

---

*General Semantics is often referred to as GS by its aficionados.

down the drain."

Taken aback, he said, "Are you sure you know what GS *is?*"

"Certainly!" she exclaimed. "Group Sex, of course."

The story—a true one—is now part of my repertoire for illustrating the point: People often attack that which they do not understand.

In the years since GS first came to public attention it has often been attacked, and many of these attacks have been almost as absurdly confused as the one by the lady at the cocktail party. Such impressionistic confusion can be expected, of course, from superficial and uneducated people. But it is surprising and rather saddening to find it in the work of a man of considerable academic stature and influence.

The case to which I refer is that of Russian-born Pitirim Sorokin, who in 1930 established a new department of sociology at Harvard University and who made of it a major center for general sociology studies. He was elected president of the International Institution of Sociology in 1936 and President of the American Sociological Association in 1964, and received many other honors.

Sorokin's work has long been a matter of controversy. Some critics have been in disagreement with his conclusions; others, merely critical of the manner in which he arrived at them.

In any case—whether General Semanticists agree or do not agree with Sorokin—his needling attacks on GS should be a matter of some concern to them inasmuch as Sorokin's written output was prodigious, and his reading public quite extensive. Several of his thirty books are regarded as classics in the field, and many of them have been translated into Japanese, Chinese, Spanish, Polish, Norwegian, Ukrainian, German, Czechoslovakian, and other languages. In fact, Sorokin has the reputation of being the world's most widely translated sociologist. His negative comments on GS can therefore be damaging if only because they could prejudice thousands of readers against investigating GS for themselves.

It soon becomes apparent to anyone who reads him that Pitirim Sorokin knew a great deal about a great many things; and—modern knowledge being as vast as it is—we really cannot expect that he should have also known a great deal about GS. However, from a man who founded and for so many years directed the Center for the Study of Creative Altruism at Harvard, one might have expected either a gentle silence on his part or a more charitable tone. But Sorokin could not seem to remain silent about GS; and he was certainly far from charitable.

The opening chapter of his well-known book, *Fads and Foibles in Modern Sociology*—a critique of contemporary research procedures—strikes the keynote of his basic attitude. The chapter is entitled "Amnesia and the New Columbuses," and its principal argument is that many modern sociologists and other researchers claim mistakenly that they have made a scientific discovery for the first time in human history, a foible which Sorokin dubbed "the obsessive discoverer's complex."

Soon thereafter he refers to Anatol Rapaport's book, *Operational Philosophy,* and denounces what Rapaport had to say about GS in the following terms:

"As a matter of fact, everything that is sound in Korzybski's semantics was very thoroughly discovered and formulated some 2,000 years ago, especially by the great Buddhist logicians: Gotama[1], Dignaga, Vasubadnhu, Dharmakirti, and by other thinkers of India, China, Greece, Rome, and Europe of the Middle Ages. Even the main motto of the contemporary semanticists, that the word is not the thing, the map is not the territory, was coined by the above-mentioned logicians. It needs no arguing that for at least two millenia epistemology has dealt with all the main problems of today's semantics, and dealt with them more completely than the modern semanticists do."[2]

In a footnote to chapter 19 in *The Ways and Power of Love* we find Sorokin making substantially the same accusation:

"Recent 'semantics' pompously claims the great discovery that 'the word is not the thing; the map is not the territory.' See R. Meyers, 'The Nervous System and General Semantics,' *ETC.*, Vol. 5, no. 4, 1948, p. 232. We see that not only the discovery but even the phrase 'the word is not the thing' was discovered some two thousand years ago."[3]

And in *SOS, The Meaning of Our Crisis,* we find:

"The so-called 'semantic' distortion and vulgarization of the work of hundreds of eminent thinkers, Oriental and Occidental, who some two thousand years ago said all the sound things that are in this semantics, and said them incomparably better—this semantics has been declared to be the epoch-making last word in

---

1. It is not clear whether Sorokin is referring here to Gautama Buddha (sometimes spelled Gotama) or to another Buddhist thinker.
2. Sorokin, Pitirim. *Fads and Foibles in Modern Sociology,* Henry Regnery Co., Chicago, 1956 pp. 7-8.
3. Sorokin, Pitirim. *The Ways and Power of Love,* The Beacon Press, Boston, 1951, p. 131.
4. Sorokin, Pitirim. *SOS, The Meaning of Our Crisis,* The Beacon Press, Boston, 1951, p. 131.

science and philosophy and scientific thought."[4]

In short, Professor Sorokin's principal quarrel with General Semantics seems to be that (1) "everything" of any value in it was formulated some 2,000 years ago; and yet (2) its proponents claim for it an originality that it does not have. It would be well to consider both these accusations.

Let us first consider the proposition: There is nothing new in General Semantics.

Would it be uncharitable to begin by pointing out that altruistic love—which was Sorokin's specialty for a number of years—was also discovered and formulated some 2,000 years ago, and, indeed, even much earlier? That not only Jesus but Gautama Buddha and other Eastern teachers taught precisely the same thing which is the principal concern of Professor Sorokin's 532-page volume, *The Ways and Power of Love?* and that they taught it much more simply and in some ways incomparably better, since what they had to say was uncluttered by arguments, accusations, footnotes, indices, documentation, and all the paraphernalia of scholarship?

As a matter of fact, if we were to approach almost anything in modern civilization in Sorokin's temper of mind we would have to come to the same damning conclusion: The ancients had some form of it also. Bathtubs? A pox on them! Pompeii had bathtubs far surpassing in elegance anything produced by Kohler or Crane. Taxicabs? Bumptious upstarts! Rome had chariots two millenia ago. Airplanes? Insolent pretenders to originality! Butterflies have been flying since the dawn of the planet.

Even if we grant, for the moment, the possibility that "everything" in GS was said centuries ago, we must point out one important fact that Sorokin seems to have overlooked. That is that truths need to be frequently restated—just as devices need to be frequently redevised—in order to fit the needs of the times and to take advantage of the new resources of the times.

In an advertising trade journal some years ago there appeared an article which made the point very tellingly. "Remember!" it said. "Every year 300,000,000 babies are born who never saw an elephant!" There could hardly be a more vivid reminder of the fact that every new generation comes to this planet ignorant of everything known to its elders and to its ancestors; and they need to be *told*. Moreover, they need to be told in the idiom of their own times.

Professor Sorokin made much of the fact that classical Buddhist thinkers had formulated the very same principles that

67

Korzybski did. Quite apart from the important question: How *many* of the Korzybskian principles did they formulate?—which must be answered *Not all of them*—and How clearly did they express them? there is another very important consideration, namely: How *accessible* are these ancient formulations to the average person of the West?

Gotama, Dignaga, Vasubandhu, and Dharmakirti may well have had superior epistemological insights as regards the map-territory idea; but their names are not even listed alphabetically in the Encyclopedia Britannica. The source book from which Sorokin apparently drew his information (Th. Tscherbatsky, *The Buddhist Logic,* Leningrad, 1932, 2 volumes) is in all probability not to be found in most American public libraries and to expect the average person to track down such a book in research libraries is to expect something far beyond the average person's time, patience, interest, and sense of what is important.

Even were you to hand him on a silver platter the source book he would need, nothing could be more unlikely than that the average person would be willing to plow through the intricacies of Eastern treatises on philosophy in order to find one morsel of epistemology that could be useful to him in his everyday living. In fact, if you were to do so much as to mention the word epistemology to him, he would probably say "Episte *Who?*"

You probably would get the same baffled expression if you mentioned the term General Semantics to many people also; the system is still not as widely known as it should be. But little by little, whether known by that name or not, GS principles are being applied in more and more places, and taught in more and more schools.

This is precisely the reason why GS is of so much value and so much importance. It is *available.* It is stated in contemporary terms, incorporating the data of modern physics. It makes accessible to people of all ranges of education and intelligence the epistmological insights that for centuries have principally been the brooding matter of philosophers. It has reduced these insights, in a *system,* to terms that a six-year-old child can understand.

If Professor Sorokin regarded this accessibility as "vulgarization," more's the pity.

Professor Sorokin was annoyed not only with the lack of "newness" in General Semantics; he was annoyed also with the "claims" that its proponents made for its originality.

It is worth reexamining in this connection the above-quoted " 'the word is not the thing; the map is not the territory.' See R.

Meyers, 'The Nervous System and General Semantics,' *ETC.*, Vol. 5, No. 4, 948, p. 232. We see that not only the discovery but even the phrase, 'the word is not the thing' was discovered some two thousand years ago."

We cannot help but note in passing that the very structure of Sorokin's first sentence ("Recent 'semantics' pompously claims") suggests that he had no conception of some of the rudiments of semantic discipline. The construction he used is a very common one in writing and speech, to be sure; all sorts of people say "Science says," "Chemistry tells us," or "History reveals"; and such phrases are a part of our linguistic habit patterns. But when we become a little more semantically aware, we realize that "science," "chemistry," "history," or "semantics," being inanimate abstractions, cannot properly be said to "say," "tell," "reveal," or "claim" anything. Only individual scientists, chemists, historians, or semanticists can do these things; and if we phrase it in the manner of Professor Sorokin, we fall into the error of "illegitimate totality," to use a good phrase of Bertrand Russell.

What Professor Sorokin probably means, of course, is that he thinks that semanticists pompously claim certain things. Since he proceeds in the next sentence to document, presumably, the first, we might find it instructive to inspect the 1948 article in *ETC.* to which Sorokin refers.

R. Meyers, as Sorokin calls him, is Russell Meyers, M.D., formerly professor of neurosurgery and head of the Department of Neurosurgery at the University of Iowa College of Medicine. A careful examination of his text in *ETC.* will show that the word *pompous* seems a singularly inappropriate adjective with which to describe the tone of the article. Moreover Dr. Meyers *nowhere makes any claim of discovery, on the part of anyone, that the word is not the thing;* he simply reports this as a premise of the General Semanticist.

He then proceeds in what seemed to the present writer a mild-mannered and simple style to establish various other points, one of the major ones being that General Semantics is concerned, among other things, with getting people to use the scientific method in everyday thinking and living. If Professor Sorokin ever read the article carefully, and in its entirety, it is certainly not apparent in either the content or the tenor of his footnote—a somewhat surprising circumstance in view of his own righteous indignation over the "brazenly unprecise" and "grossly unscientific" statements of a certain sociologist whose work he flails in *Fads and Foibles in Modern Sociology.*

If Professor Sorokin had spent a little more time in actually studying the elementary principles of GS and a little less time in denouncing them as old hat, he might have been acquainted with a little Korzybskian device, called indexing—a device, incidentally, which so far as we can tell never occurred to the Buddhist logicians of 2,000 years ago. He would have then realized that semanticist$_1$ is not semanticist$_2$ is not semanticist$_3$; which simply says in a rather mathematical way that not all semanticists are alike. If Sorokin had grasped this simple basic idea his mind might then have been sufficiently uncluttered by prejudice to read dispassionately a few other semanticists besides R. Meyers—K. Keyes, for example, or I. Lee, or W. Johnson, or S. Hayakawa—and conceivably he might have discovered that not all semanticists are pompous.

He might even have gone so far as to read A. Korzybski and to look up in *Science and Sanity* the passages dealing with the map-territory idea. Had he done so, it is quite true that he would not have found Korzybski making any allusions to the Buddhist thinkers.[5] But neither would he have found him making any claims, pompous or otherwise, that he had discovered the map-territory idea.

He could also, had he browsed through the book, conceivably have found many passages which are singularly unpretentious. Although Korzybski made a number of important and provocative formulations, and introduced a new terminology justified by the freshness of his approach, again and again he disclaims absolute finality to absolute originality for his system. Here are a few examples, taken from the third edition:

"The present inquiry is limited and partial. . . ."[6]

"This work is not exhaustive in any field; nor, at the present, can it be."[7]

"Now I present the results of this work to the public. It is the best I can do, although I fully realize its limitations and imperfections."[8]

"One of the dangers into which the reader is liable to fall is to ascribe too much generality to the work, to forget the limitations, and perhaps, the one-sidedness which underlie it."[9]

---

5. It is possible that Korzybski knew about Eastern concepts and their correlations with his own work, but did not mention them because he wanted his work to be accepted on its own merits by the scientific world.
6. Korzybski, Alfred. *Science and Sanity,* The International Non-Aristotelian Publishing Co., 4th edition, 1958, p. 10.
7. Ibid, p. 16.
8. Ibid, p. 44.
9. Ibid, p. 143.

It seems a pity that Professor Sorokin never read—or if he did read, did not remember—a very important little sentence that Korzybski wrote in the introduction to the second edition of *Science and Sanity* which reads as follows:

"The separate issues involved in GS are not entirely new; their methodological formulation *as a system* which is workable, teachable, and so elementary it can be applied by children, is entirely new."[10]

If, in the face of all this evidence, Sorokin still could insist on calling Korzybski and/or semanticists "pompous," it might have been well to tell him that we can easily think of some pompous proponents of Christianity and of brotherly love. But the pomposity of the proponent, fortunately, has nothing to do with the merits of the system otherwise. We have even known pompous salesmen of Buicks. This cast no reflection, however, on the merits of the Buick; it only proves that the salesmen in question were pompous.

As a matter of fact, the General Semantics discipline by its very nature tends to *reduce* the pretensions of people. By and large, semanticists are *less* likely to be guilty of this human failing than the followers of many other systems of thinking, both religious and scientific. Any students who really grasps the idea of non-allness could hardly help but lose some of his former complacency and self-importance if he had any. One of the first things we learn in GS is that all of us, being human, have a limited awareness mechanism, and therefore we can never grasp *all* of reality; we can know it only in part.

If Professor Sorokin had only learned—and applied—this elementary general semantics principle which high school students are learning to apply in those schools which are so enlightened as to teach it, he would have expressed himself on many occasions in far less absolute terms, and he would not have blundered so badly and in so unscholarly a manner with regard to General Semantics itself.

What is equally as unfortunate is that, in his prejudicial haze of outrage, Sorokin missed the fact that GS constitutes a highly important ally to his own major concern in the latter portion of his life.

Though Sorokin and Korzybski differed widely at many points, there are a number of interesting parallels between them. Both were born of Slavic origins near the end of the last century, within nine years of each other; both came to this country and

---

10. Ibid, p xxvii.

mastered the English language well enough to do much of their productive work in that language. Both had considerable erudition in a variety of fields; both had firsthand experience with the barbarities of revolution or of war. Both were appalled by the spectacle of human behavior, individually and collectively, and both were convinced that this was a time of unprecedented crisis in human history. Both dedicated themselves with indefatigable labors to the amelioration of the future of humanity.

Korzybski once said jocularly in a seminar lecture: "I began to study the state of the world. I found that it wasn't bad. It was hopeless." Actually, however, Korzybski was not really without hope about the state of the world—or at least, his positive, dynamic, perseverance through the years did not bespeak true hopelessness; and neither did Sorokin seem so, for the same reason. However outraged they both may have been at the deterioration of human values and the spectacle of human idiocy, both had hope that there was a way out of the mess we are in, and that there could result from the debacle of our current civilization a finer and healthier society through the introduction of new elements.

It was in their analysis of the reasons for the present crisis, and their proposals for the manner in which it could be salvaged or transformed, that they differed so completely.

The great divergence between their approaches may in part be explainable by the divergence of their backgrounds. Korzybski was an engineer and a mathematician; Sorokin was not. Korzybski was acutely aware of linguistic and symbolic factors in the human situation; Sorokin, apparently, was not.

In 1948 Eli Lilly offered to sponsor Sorokin's studies in "How to make human beings less selfish and more creative," and the Lilly endowment fund made possible the establishment of the Harvard Center for the study of Creative Altruism which Sorokin directed for twelve years. *Creative altruism* was the term chosen to substitute for the word *love,* which Sorokin felt was tarnished by much misuse.

Korzybski seemed to have been chary of the word *love: Science and Sanity* mentions it only a few times; and the words *brotherhood* and *altruism* do not even appear in the index. And yet the whole thrust of the GS system is to make people less judgmental and therefore more loving; less likely to make wild and irresponsible inferences, and therefore more brotherly; more conscious of their ethical and social obligations as time-binders, and therefore more altruistic.

How unfortunate that Sorokin—instead of fulminating about how ancient the map-territory idea was, and how conceited the General Semanticists were for thinking they had discovered it— did not actually go to the territory of GS practice rather than depend on his own impressionistic and hasty look at a few of its maps! Had he done so, his readers would have been spared the badly distorted and inadequate maps he himself made about GS, and people in many countries of the world would have been more accurately informed of a very valuable resource for the solution of the urgent problems which face us all.

PART III:
TWO UNUSUAL RELIGIONS

Though I am of Italian descent, I was not raised, as people often assume, in the Catholic faith. They also seem surprised to discover that I don't like spaghetti—but stereotypes die very hard.

My father's mother hoped that he would become a priest, and she sent him to a seminary in Italy. He had disillusioning experiences there, which left him something of an agnostic as regards religion. He came to this country as a boy of seventeen, put himself through law school at the University of Wisconsin, became a successful lawyer and the Italian consul in Milwaukee, a diplomatic post he held for more than twenty-five years.

My mother was a perennial student of religions and movements of all kinds, and for a long period of time faithfully attended meetings of the Theosophical Society in Milwaukee, where we lived. So I was raised largely in a Theosophical tradition.

It might be worth noting, for those who happen to be unacquainted with the Theosophical Society, that its three main objectives are as follows:

(1) to form a nucleus of universal brotherhood without distinction of race, creed, color, or sex;

(2) to study the hidden laws of nature (among which are included, principally, reincarnation and karma) and the powers latent in man (telepathy, clairvoyance, etc.)

and (3) to make comparative studies of religion, science, and philosophy.

When one considers that these objectives were formulated in

75

1875 by its two founders, Mme. Blavatsky and Colonel Olcott, in an era of racial and national provincialism, an era of very rigid and self-righteous religious orthodoxy, and an era of deeply entrenched materialistic science, one can appreciate how courageous and ahead of their times the founders were.

All of these objectives, which were often discussed in the Theosophical Lodge I attended, affected my outlook as I was growing up. Racial prejudice was a matter of great concern to me, and resulted in innumerable activist experiences which came to fruition in a book I wrote called *The Mark Twain Proposition*—a comic yet serious novel on the subject. Reincarnation and karma also concerned me, and resulted in my two books on the Cayce material, *Many Mansions* and *The World Within,* and their sequel, *Many Lives, Many Loves.* As for religion, comparative religion always interested me, and for a year or so, I tried to go to a different church or temple every week by way of exploring various approaches.

I never wrote many articles on the subject of religion—in fact, only the two which follow here—and I wrote only one book about it, *Insights For the Age of Aquarius,* which I have already referred to. I also included it as a subsidiary theme in *The Mark Twain Proposition* in the character of Elwood Trumble, who was writing a book called *Christianity's Calamitous Confusions.* Using the tools of General Semantics, I have been critical of religion, but constructively so, in both these books.

BAHAI: THE RELIGION THAT PRACTICES AND TEACHES RACIAL EQUALITY

The Bahai faith was of interest to me for some time and I used to attend its meetings in Milwaukee and Madison. My college friend (referred to as "Lola" in the piece I wrote about her—"The Pen Can Be Dangerous as the Sword") was an ardent Bahai and we used to have long discussions on the subject.

I am not usually a joiner of organizations and probably would not have become a Bahai anyway; but there were several distinct reasons for my special reluctance in this case. One was what seemed to me a very curious discrepancy.

One of the twelve Bahai principles is: "The independent investigation of truth"—a principle stated in a religious context and intended to mean that in the new age people should not believe a dogma just because they are told to believe it. An admirable principle, I think. Yet when you raise the question of reincarnation to nine out of ten Bahais, they will tell you flatly that they don't believe it because on page something of one of their basic books Bahaullah says it isn't so—which hardly seems like independent investigation to me. I have met a few Bahais who in the spirit of investigation have examined the evidence for reincarnation and have come to accept it—rationalizing their position by saying that Bahaullah himself probably believed it, but felt at the time he was writing that it would be unwise to raise still another controversial issue.

At any rate I did not become a Bahai, and used to tell Lola: "You take the Bahai way and I'll take the Balow way and I'll get to heaven afore ye."

At the present time (1983) under the Ayatollah Khomeini's regime in Iran, thousands of Bahais have been tortured and executed and their property confiscated for being "heretics" and for "spreading corruption." In a village near Birjaud a Bahai husband and wife were tied to the door of their home; wood was piled over them, and a fire was set, burning them to death. Bahai women—because they reject the veil and participate with their husbands and brothers in administering community affairs—have been labeled "prostitutues," and their children, called "illegitimate" and denied access to education. Bahai cemeteries have been vandalized and bulldozed; the beautiful Bahai shrines, temples, and gardens have been demolished and parking lots made of some of the sites. Even legal emigration is made impossible, and some Bahais who have managed to leave the country illegally have been apprehended and their passports canceled.

It is truly sad to note that the fury of religious hatred in this world seems never to abate.

This article was published in a magazine called Negro Digest, *in September 1949., The magazine is now defunct—or, as a doctor I know used to write it, defunked. He doctored better than he spelled.*

Bahai.

The name rather suggests a flamboyant town in Brazil. But it refers instead to a religion whose followers not only believe in, but actually practice, racial equality.

It would be impossible to find a segretated Bahai congregation, even in the state of Georgia. For from its very beginning, 100 years ago in Persia, the Bahai religion has explicitly taught the equality of all colors and races of people. "Ye are all flowers in the garden of God," proclaimed Baha-ullah, the founder of the faith. "It is the variety of the garden that makes it so beautiful. Were it of one color alone, it would not have such splendour."

The writings of Baha-ullah abound in similarly poetic comparisons. "The peoples of the world are leaves of one tree and fruits of one orchard." "In the clustered jewels of the races, the colored peoples are as sapphires and rubies, the white as diamonds and pearls. The composite beauty of humanity will be seen only in their unity and their blending."

But the comparisons are merely illustrations of one of the twelve cardinal principles of the faith: namely, the oneness of mankind and the equality of all its peoples.

Whatever final evaluation time may place on the merits of the Bahai faith in the history of religion, there is little doubt that above all religions it stands as a paragon in genuine practice of its principles. It is an unmistakable influence for the furtherance of the cause of the American Negro in his struggle for full emancipation.

Bahais, in every one of the ninety-three countries in which the faith has taken root, practice racial equality not only in their spiritual assemblies, but also in their affairs of everyday life. This is true even in the southern states of this country, though, as might be expected, Bahai followers are more numerous in the North. California has the greatest number of assemblies with thirty; then follows Illinois with sixteen; Michigan with twelve; New Jersey with ten; and New York with nine. But all of the southern states are represented—Florida and Missouri being in the lead with three assemblies each; South Carolina, Tennessee, Virginia, and Georgia following with two apiece; and Alabama, Kentucky, North Carolina, Louisiana, Oklahoma, and West Virginia having one apiece.

As in the case of Buddha and Christ (*Buddha* meaning "The Enlightened One" and *Christ* meaning "The Anointed One"), the name of Baha-ullah is not the given name of the founder, but rather a title bestowed on him by his followers. In the Persian language, the word means "The Glory of God"; "Bahai," then, simply means a follower of Baha-ullah.

A young prophet who called himself the Bab, or the Gate, was the forerunner of Baha-ullah. In 1844 the Bab began to go about Persia teaching that there would soon appear among them a great world teacher whose mission it would be to unite the peoples of the world and usher in a new era of peace and enlightenment. The Bab won many enthusiastic followers, more than twenty thousand of which were finally massacred by the Islamic clergy and the Persian government: the Bab himself died a martyr's death in 1850.

In 1863 Baha-ullah announced himself to the few remaining followers of the Bab as the teacher that had been prophesied. The force of both his personality and his message soon attracted many people; and once again persecution was directed against the new teaching. Baha-ullah was arrested, deprived of his rights and possessions, exiled, and finally imprisoned for life in a Turkish penal colony at the foot of Mt. Carmel in the Holy Land, where he died, after twenty-four years of imprisonment, in 1892. During the period of his imprisonment he expounded, in some one hundred volumes, the principles of the religion which is now known as the Bahai World Faith and which today seems to be one of the few unifying forces in a world torn by so many disunities. Christians, Moslems, Jews, Hindus, Buddhists, and Zoroastrians have become adherents of the Bahai teachings; they do not thereby reject their own original faith, but merely acknowledge that it is but one of the many possible pathways to God.

The Bahai point of view on religion is this: from time to time there has appeared on earth some divinely inspired person (or "Manifestation of God") like Krishna or Buddha or Christ, who reveals spiritual truths to a portion of mankind. All of these great teachers have taught the same essential truths about the same God, though He has naturally been called by different names in different languages. Moreover the teachers of necessity adapted these truths to meet the needs of the people in the particular country and the particular era of history in which they lived. With the passing of centuries, rituals and dogmas grew up which had little or no genuine connection with the original teachings of the founder; consequently the religions of the world as we know them today seem to differ completely from one another, even though at their point of origin they were all essentially the same. These apparent differences are thus the cause of much unnecessary prejudice, hatred, and strife.

Stripped of the gradual accretions and distortions of their followers, however, and stripped also of the peculiar rules and regulations having to do with a particular time and place in history, all religions are, says Baha-ullah, essentially the same truth differently expressed. They may be regarded as different facets, or different emphases, of the same great principles which relate man to God and to the moral order of the universe.

Religion in this distilled and universal sense is, then, according to Baha-ullah, the only possible basis for a truly civilized community of human beings. Since all men are children of the same Divine Father they are consequently all brothers to one another. This brotherhood or Oneness of mankind thus becomes the pivot around which all the teachings of the faith revolve. "The earth is but one country," wrote Baha-ullah, "and mankind its citizens." Again: "The lovers of mankind, these are the superior men, of whatever nation, creed, or color they may be!. . . .God is no respecter of persons on account of either color or race. . . .Inasmuch as all were created in the image of God, we must bring ourselves to realize that all embody divine possibilities."

It will be noted that this is the first religion in the known history of the world which explicitly declares the equality of woman to man. All previous religious systems placed men above women, not usually because of the teachings of the founder himself, but because of the cultural interpretations placed upon the teaching by the people who surrounded and followed him. It will also be noted that—though all other religions imply human brotherhood through their commandments that men love one another—this is the first religion which explicitly states that all races of people are equal.

Undoubtedly the absence of explicit references to the matter of race equality in the great scriptures of the world is due to the fact that it is only recently that race and nationality have become so paramount an issue in men's minds. Cultural forces—particularly the expansion of rapid means of transportation and the resultant breakdown of ancient national isolations—have now caused the problem to become paramount in the political and ethical situation of the world; hence the peculiar force of Baha-ullah's teachings with regard to it.

Other interesting aspects of the Bahai faith are the absence of a professional clergy; they have teachers, but no paid ministers or priests who hold their offices for life. Unlike most other religions, also, it is forbidden in the Bahai faith to proselyte, or seek to make converts. Teachers who go out voluntarily to spread the faith receive no pay and support themselves in other ways while on their teaching mission.

The headquarters of the Bahai faith in America is located in Wilmette, a suburb of Chicago. Here stands a million-dollar temple the erection of which was financed entirely by the voluntary contributions of the followers. The temple—a visit to which is now included on the itinerary of most bus tours of Chicago—is a beautiful circular structure having nine entrances and nine aisles leading to the center. This is symbolic of the Bahai teaching that the nine great world religions are all pathways to God. On the outer columns of the building there are religious symbols drawn from all the major religions of the world, including the six-pointed star of Judaism, the cross of Christianity, and the star and crescent of Islam. They are placed in rising chronological order, to indicate the continuity of religious truth throughout the ages. Above them all is a nine-pointed star to symbolize the coming religious unity of the human race.

In other towns of the United States, however, the meeting places of the Bahais are far more humble. Usually, where the membership is large enough to warrant it, a room or suite of rooms is rented in some downtown office building. Here there are held the weekly public meetings and the monthly religious feasts which, according to the Bahai calendar of nineteen months with nineteen days each, falls on the nineteenth day of each month. Fireside meetings and study groups supplement the public meetings. These are usually held in private homes and their object is to study more thoroughly the teachings of the faith in all its religious and sociological aspects.

Thousands of Negroes in the United States have become members of the Bahai faith. An exact census of their number is not available since Bahais do not consider it important to make a distinction between white and black persons. But it is apparent to anyone who attends a local Bahai assembly meeting, or a national conference at the temple in Wilmette, that Negroes are well-represented numerically, and that they are accepted unselfconsciously and without patronage as equals.

In many cases this attitude on the part of white members has been consciously and painfully acquired. This is particularly true in the case of white Southerners, who have been attracted to the faith for its One-World unifying outlook or for other of its basic tenets, and then find themselves faced with the necessity of accepting also the tenet of the equality of all races. For such people a Bahai meeting is their first experience in meeting a Negro as a social equal; the process of gradually adjusting their ingrained habit patterns to the ideology of their new faith is not always an easy one.

DISCOVERING JAPAN— AND SHINTO

This article, in a slightly longer form, was written (on request) during my stay in Japan and it was published in Japanese translation in a Japanese magazine the name of which eludes me. Japanese script is beautiful to look at, but for me at least, impossible to comprehend.

If Americans generally have difficulty in learning Japanese (and almost invariably they do), it is fully matched by the difficulty Japanese have in learning English. I began to realize this fact while on the Japanese plane going to Tokyo. There was a small sign over one of the water dispensers which read: "Out of work."

I went to Japan because I was invited there by the publisher of Many Mansions *in Japanese translation. He wanted me to give lectures by way of publicizing the book. It turned out to be an exciting but strenuous experience.*

I have made many journeys in my life, and most of them were meaningful to me in one way or another. However, my trip to Japan in the fall of 1971 was in many ways more rewarding— aesthetically, intellectually, and spiritually—than any previous trip I had ever taken.

As with most American tourists, my first stop was in Tokyo. In some respects a stay in Tokyo is no different from one in New York, Chicago, or any other big western city. Tokyo has subways and freeways, traffic jams and exhaust fumes, skyscrapers and perpetual road construction, abominable drinking water, smog, and deafening noise. Yet somehow there is a difference. Despite all the devices and disadvantages of modern technology, Tokyo—and all Japan, as I soon found—retains a distinctive Japanese quality not to be found elsewhere on this planet.

Two of the things which particularly impressed me were the use of *oshiboris* and the custom of taking off one's shoes when entering a house. The *oshibori* is a rolled-up, hot, wet towel—a little larger, usually, than an American face cloth—which is served to patrons in restaurants or guests in a home before they start to eat or to drink tea, and on trains and planes shortly after the journey begins. Usually the *oshibori* is served in a small wicker receptacle designed for the purpose. Both on hot days and cold, it is a welcome and refreshing comfort, which I for one would like to see other countries adopt. As for taking off one's shoes before entering a house, this is a uniquely Japanese and sensible custom. Why should one track the dirt and grime of the street inside to the place where one lives? The common denominator of both these customs is, of course, the Japanese love of cleanliness.

Another distinctive aspect of Japan that delighted me early in my stay was the beauty of the paper in which purchases are wrapped. Colorful, imaginative designs characterize the wrapping paper of almost all the shops; and I found it difficult, in fact, impossible, to discard them. My luggage on the trip home was considerably heavier than before, not only because of the purchases I had made and the gifts I had received, but because of the collection of wrapping paper I had accumulated.

Then there is the Japanese love of flowers. In Japan many taxi drivers and bus drivers have a small vase on their dashboard, containing one or two blossoms. (Imagine, if you can, a New York taxi driver with a bud vase on his dashboard!) On Japanese television (I wish some of its lively and colorful variety shows would be shown in this country) I frequently saw that the singer had attached a fresh flower to the microphone that she (or he) held close to the face while singing. And in almost every home there is a *tokonoma*—a small space in a room, elevated a few inches from the floor, in front of which an honored guest is seated. On the wall behind the raised space is hung a painting or a piece of calligraphy, and on the floor is a vase with a single flower or a beautiful group of flowers, arranged according to the ancient Japanese art of flower arranging.

The Japanese, in short, are an artistic people, sensitive to the beauty of nature, and enormously gifted in giving expression to this beauty in many ways.

It was on this trip that I became acutely aware of the fact that these expressions of cleanliness, artistry, and nature appreciation were not isolated or unrelated phenomena, but rather were deeply rooted in the Japanese religious outlook on life.

This outlook is a composite of Buddhism, which was imported from India by way of China in the fourth century, and Shinto, which was the more ancient, native faith. It would probably be very difficult to say which of the two has had the greater effect upon the Japanese character—as difficult as to say whether the sun or the rain has had more effect upon a cherry orchard. But I would suspect that Shinto has been deeper and more all-pervasive.

Buddhism, of course, has become fairly well known to Westerners in recent years, especially through the practice of Zen. But Shinto has not. I must confess to an almost total ignorance of it myself until I visited Japan.

Shintoism has perhaps been less accessible to Westerners because its scriptures (the *Kojiki* and the *Nihonshoki*) are filled with a complicated mythology and numerous elaborate and fanciful prayers. They are not as readable or intelligible to foreigners as the usually lucid and rational (if sometimes repetitious) Buddhist scriptures. One needs to seek out the ideas of Shinto in places other than their sacred books.

Unfortunately, we are likely to get a very negative impression of it if we examine recent history. What we need to remember is that Shinto, like all other religions, can be and has been badly misused; and we need to recall that in Christian history, the monstrous cruelties of the Inquisition were justified by their perpetrators on the grounds of scriptural passages and the defending of the purity of the faith. Burning at the stake, for example, was justified on the basis of an obscure Bible passage prohibiting the shedding of blood, and confiscating all the possessions and property of heretics was justified on the basis of Adam and Eve being banished from the Garden of Eden after the "fall."

In Japan there was no Inquisition, but the twisting of ideas in one major instance was equally as perverse. Just previous to and during World War II, the creation myth of Shinto was adapted by militarists to support nationalism and wars of conquest. The idea that they seized upon was that the Japanese islands were a special creation of the Sun-god and the Sun-goddess, and that the emperor was their divine descendant. This essentially folkloric idea was regarded as a divine sanction for global expansion and the infallibility of the emperor—an idea which flourished until Japan's defeat in 1945. Shortly after this defeat, the emperor disavowed his divine descent, and his right to command wars of conquest, and Shinto reverted to its previous gentle, unaggressive, and spiritual form.

From its earliest beginnings, Shinto has taught that the entire universe is filled with spirit. *Kami Nagara*—"Whatever is, is Divine Spirit"—is its core concept. This is not a mere poetic or mystical phrase with the Japanese. It has a daily and immediate practical reality. The flowers of the field, the fruits of the orchard, the forests, the crops, the soil, the waters, the mountains, the stones—all are expressions of divine spirit. To this spirit and all its manifestations, we owe our very life, and therefore we owe them our respect and our *gratitude*.*

So far as I could tell, Shinto has nothing to say about social action or service; nor does it have any ethical commandments. But with the core concept of *Everything is Divine Spirit,* a reverent and gentle behavior toward all living creatures naturally follows, as does an alert interest in every aspect of life, a sense of the inter-relatedness of everything in the universe, and the use of nature motifs in every art form, even the most utilitarian.

In addition, Shinto has other simple talismanic concepts. Sincerity. Purity. Everlasting industriousness and creativeness. Duty to the ancestors. Co-operation with the god-beings who govern the growing of plant life on this planet. It is no wonder that Japan is, in a very real sense, a nation of gardeners! But with them gardening is not merely a trade or a hobby; it is a spiritual outlook on the nature of the world.

All these concepts came to life for me in Japan as I visited gardens and spoke to Japanese people; but they became especially vivid when I visited the great Shinto shrine in the town of Ise, about three hours away by train from Tokyo. According to tradition, the shrine was founded in the year 4 B.C. It is set in a huge grove of ancient trees, and the grounds include some 1,500 acres of land. Seeing the majesty of the great, towering trees, I could not help but think of the lines of the American poet, William Cullen Bryant: "The groves were God's first temples."

Most of the symbolism of the shrine's beautiful gardens and buildings has to do with the ideas of purification and renewal. Before entering the grounds, everyone must wash his hands and rinse his mouth; a large basin of water with wooden dippers is provided at the entrance for this purpose. Other and more

---

*The similarity between the Shinto outlook and that of the American Indian is striking. This becomes apparent in reading *The Gospel of the Red Man, An Indian Bible,* by Ernest Thompson Seton (American nature writer and founder of the Boy Scouts of America) (Doubleday, Doran, and Co., 1926) and the biography of Rolling Thunder, well-known Cherokee medicine man, by Doug Boyd. (*Rolling Thunder,* Random House, N.Y., 1974)

elaborate ceremonies of purification—by water, air, and fire—are enacted before the pilgrims may enter the Outer Court and the Inner Court. Renewal is symbolized in many ways, the most astonishing one (to me) being the fact that every twenty years, the entire main building—a large, solidly built, elaborately decorated structure—is completely taken down and an exact replica is built, down to the minutest detail, on an alternate and adjoining site. Even more astonishing to me was the account given to me by the young Shinto priest who accompanied me through the gardens about how the lumber is obtained. He told me that an expedition is made into the mountain forests by the priests, who conduct a special ceremony before lumbermen fell the trees. One of the priests says a prayer to the spirit of the mountain and to the spirit of one of the gigantic trees, taken as representative for all of them. It is a prayer for forgiveness for the taking of its life. "We are going to cut you down, O tree. Forgive us, please. We do not kill you just to kill you. Your body will be used to house the sacred symbols and to remind us of the sacredness of all that lives."

Ten years ago I might have thought this beautiful and poetic but perhaps a bit excessive. Now, in the light of the Cleve Backster experiments* showing that plants have memory, feeling, intelligence, and even, apparently, ESP, I do not find it excessive at all. I find it, rather, an intelligent, courteous, and appropriate thing to do. I even have a fantasy that some day every land-developer and road builder in the world will say a similar prayer before cutting anything down, and will refrain, out of spiritual conviction, from the unnecessary destruction of any tree or other living thing. . . . The fantasy no doubt belongs in the same bracket of Really Remote Possibilities with the fantasy that every New York taxi driver will one day have a bud vase on his dashboard.

I would like to have spent three months in Japan rather than the three weeks that I did. Though the country, with all its islands, comprises an area less than the area of the state of California, three years would not have been enough to exhaust its religions and religious resources. Christopher Marlowe's phrase, "Infinite riches in a little room" comes to mind to describe it. Japan's natural beauty is magical. Its cultural heritage is enormous. To be sure, there is an unmistakable materialism and aimlessness in some of its people, typical of twentieth-century people everywhere. But at the same time there is an equally unmistakable earnestness about

---

*See *The Secret Life of Plants,* by Peter Tompkins and Christopher Bird, Harper & Row, 1973, chapter 1

most of them, an earnestness with which they pursue excellence in every field. I was impressed by their industry, their artistry, their intelligence, and their charm.

Perhaps the deepest impression I carried home with me, however, was the beauty of the Shinto faith which has so effectively molded the national character.

It is an ancient faith, mixed with fancy and myth and superstition, as are other ancient faiths. Some of its festivals and its observances would be meaningful only to native-born Japanese, and therefore could hardly be exported to other lands. But its basic idea: *Kami Nagara*—"Whatever is, is Divine Spirit"—and its other essential ideas—purification, renewal, sincerity, cleanliness, gratitude, respect for life, co-operation with the forces of nature—are peculiarly appropriate to the ecological and moral crisis of our society today. I wish they would become better known all over the world.

PART IV:
CATS AND OTHER FUR PERSONS

My mother's family came from Venice—a city famous for its picturesque canals, gondolas, and palazzi, but not so well known for the fact that it harbors thousands of cats. I discovered this when I graduated from college and my father gave me a trip to Italy by way of a graduation present. I spent several weeks in Venice, staying with a family that like many other Venetian families had three cats, and I remember playing a game with myself, as I explored the city, called Count the Cats. It consisted in seeing how many cats I could count on any single piazza, and I remember that on one of them I counted seventeen. I also remember seeing cats sitting undisturbed on cash registers or counters in little shops, cats sitting on the wide balustrades of bridges, cats looking down from balconies, and one little kitten sitting placidly in the middle of a busy street (there are no automobiles in Venice) as pedestrians walked carefully around him.

Human nature being what it is, I would imagine that there are cats in Venice who are abandoned, abused, or otherwise mistreated just as in other cities of the world; but I have the impression that Venetians for the most part are cat lovers—perhaps originally because they needed cats to fend off the water rats, but certainly now also because of simple affection.

Without needing to invoke any possible incarnation in ancient Egypt, then, I can say that I have come by my love for cats very respectably. As a child I always had one or two, and as an adult the number has varied from one to a number I sometimes refuse to disclose.

In recent years, however, my private and personal love for cats has broadened into the realization of a much larger issue—namely the relationship of the human race to the whole animal kingdom.

The following articles all deal with this realization in one way or another.

A NEW AQUARIAN AGE CONCERN: THE OTHER KINGDOMS OF LIFE

It is the view of William Irvine Thompson, the cultural historian, that the next quarter century will see the destructuring of civilization, but not its apocalyptic destruction; and that the Age of Chaos we are now entering precedes a new Age of the Gods—a time in which art, science, and religion will converge. I would like to agree with Thompson, and I would like to believe that this new convergence will include a new consciousness of our relatedness to each other and to all other living beings on this planet.

The title of his book, Darkness and Scattered Light, *seems to me an apt metaphor for our present situation. We are surrounded by darkness and evil that seems to be deepening: to read the papers, every day, and follow the news on television, contributes to a sense of despair. I remember a quip of Bob Hope on one of his TV specials. He was interviewing a college football player who practiced meditation. "Does it help you?" asked Bob. "Oh, yes," said the athlete. "It gives me a sense of peace and security, a feeling that all's right with the world." "That's funny," said Bob. "I get the same feeling just by skipping the six o'clock news!"*

In the prevailing darkness, however, there does seem to be a scattering of points of light. Places in big cities where kindness is practiced and food is given to the hungry, like St. Anthony's in San Francisco and Father Quinlan's Soup Kitchen in Norfolk. Places where homeless and abused cats are sheltered and given loving care, like Sister Seraphim's Hermitage in Tucson, Arizona, or like Mrs. Briggs's Peace Plantation in Leesburg, Virginia, where cats and dogs are given refuge. Organizations, like the ones listed at the end of the following article, which fight with single-minded devotion for the cause of those who cannot speak for themselves. Groups—like meditation and study groups I have visited in the teeming city of Tokyo or in a remote castle, sixty miles outside of Dublin—where people discuss and disseminate ideas that are no longer trammeled by orthodoxy. People who singly, and without organizational help, devote their lives to some altruistic concern. I see all these as points of light, shining bravely and alone, here and

91

there, all over the planet.

The movie industry is not generally the place to look for light of this kind. It is too much governed by motives of profit, too much impelled by the desire to entertain (for profit) and to exploit the sensation-hungry interests of the populace. The result is movies which, for the most part, are becoming more and more decadent, demonstrating Pitirim Sorokin's contention that we are in a Sensate cycle of culture, of deepening vulgarity, crudeness, and violence. A little over ten years ago two movies appeared, however, which seemed to me to be points of light in the sense that I have been discussing. I was so much impressed by them that I wrote the following article—here somewhat expanded—which was published in January 1971 in a small publication of the Inner Wisdom Foundation called The Voice. *Both these movies are, in my opinion, classics. They deserve to be revived and re-issued because they may speak now, more clearly than before, to a whole new generation of viewers, more in tune with the New Age that, I still hope, is coming into being.*

The state of public taste being what it is, it is perhaps not surprising that two extraordinary New Age movies were not great box office successes. Their poor financial showing was—according to rumor, at least—largely responsible for Darryl Zanuck, Jr., being fired by his father from 20th Century-Fox. The two movies I refer to were *On A Clear Day You Can See Forever* and *Dr. Dolittle.* Both of them were musicals; both were lavishly and imaginatively produced; both contained a powerful message.

On A Clear Day You Can See Forever concerned a psychically gifted young woman who could talk to flowers and make them grow; foresee the future; clairvoyantly find missing objects; and, under hypnosis, relive vividly a past incarnation in England.

Dr. Dolittle—a character created by Hugh Lofting while an officer in the trenches in Flanders during World War I, in a series of letters home to his children—was a veterinary doctor who loved animals deeply and learned to talk to at least 498 different species of them. "If I Could Talk To The Animals"—a delightful song sung in the movie by Rex Harrison as Dr. Dolittle—became a popular hit, often sung by Sammy Davis, Jr., and is well known to millions who never saw the movie. "If I could talk to the animals, Just imagine it, Chatting with a chimp in Chimpanzee, Imagine talking to a tiger, Chatting with a cheetah, What a neat achievement it would be!"

But there were two other distinguished songs which made a New Age point almost completely lost on the critics, many of whom dismissed the whole movie as something to sit through with the children and nothing more.

The first one was "The Vegetarian," a song in which

Dr. Dolittle tells how he refrains from eating meat ("I don't even eat horse radish!") but how occasionally he is tempted at the thought of a sausage or a steak. Then he sees his friend the pig or the cow and he knows he could not eat them; so he admits to being a "reluctant but sincere" vegetarian.

The other one is "Like Animals": a song which he sings when he is being tried for insanity on the grounds that he treats animals as if they were people. "I do not understand the human race," he begins. "It has so little love for creatures of a different face. Treating animals like people is no madness or disgrace! I do not understand the human race." He goes on: "I wonder: Why do we treat animals like animals? Animals treat us so very well! The devoted way they serve us, and protect us when we're nervous, Oh, they really don't deserve us; All we give *them* is hell!"

Leslie Bricusse, the gifted writer of the screenplay, the music, and the lyrics of all the songs in *Dr. Dolittle,* has in this song made a wise and witty statement of an important New Age awareness. We all need to learn to treat animals with the same consideration that we would give our friends. We must stop treating them like *things,* to be used callously for our own profit or pleasure.

Many persons in the various metaphysical movements have become somewhat aware of the emerging ecological concept of treating other kingdoms of nature as friends through that small classic by J. Allen Boone called *Kinship with all Life.* Boone's discovery that the movie dog Strongheart could pick up his thoughts telepathically led him to the realization that all animal life is conscious, aware, and deserving of respect. His ever-widening experiences with Strongheart and other animals led him to the additional realization that we human beings have much to learn from animals—even including rattlesnakes and those much-maligned creatures, skunks. His newfound ability to rid his house of the ants, politely but firmly, by asking them to leave, has led many persons of my acquaintance, and probably many more that I do not know about, to try the same method with equal success. Violent and cruel methods of extermination are not necessary, and in fact are often short-sighted and eventually harmful to ourselves, as in the case of DDT and other powerful insecticides.

Kinship With All Life was first published in 1954 and is still being reprinted, so its influence can be considered fairly pervasive. But the general public, including the metaphysical or "New Age" groups, are still for the most part unaware of or indifferent to the full extent of man's inhumanity to the animal kingdom. Rodeos are widely regarded as good, clean fun; most people do not know of the use of electric prods and other cruelties that go on routinely behind the scenes. Zoos are considered a pleasant way of spending an afternoon; few people think of the meaningless existence of the imprisoned animals, who pace back and forth for a lifetime, often all alone, in their small, barren cages.

Perhaps the worst of all abuses, however, is the practice of experimenting on live animals, often unanesthetized, in laboratories.

One aspect of this—and there are others, even more incredibly cruel—is toxicity testing, which causes indescribable, prolonged agony to millions of dogs, cats, rats, and primates. Standard animal tests for toxicity include force-feeding enormous amounts of the chemical under investigation, such as household cleaning products, automotive fluids and lubricants, food additives, hair dyes, etc., etc., to assess the dosage required to kill fifty percent of the animals. This is called the LD_{50}, or Lethal Dose for half the animals tested. A variation of this involves scraping off layers of the skin, applying the test chemical directly to the abraded flesh, and determining the concentration and exposure time required to kill fifty percent of the animals.

Women spend millions of dollars annually on cosmetics, not knowing, most of them, of the Draize Rabbit Tests, in which rows upon rows of rabbits are strapped into small confining stalls. Into their eyes are sprayed hormones, hair dyes, hair sprays, shampoos, and perfumes in order to test their irritancy. Since rabbits have no tear ducts, this is an excruciatingly painful experience for them. They often scream in pain or break their backs in a desperate but futile effort to break away. For up to three weeks they are restrained in the stocks, while their pus-filled eyes slowly and agonizingly ulcerate.

That so cruel a method of testing chemicals and cosmetics should be considered justifiable and, indeed, beyond question, by scientists and manufacturers, and go unprotested by lawmakers, laymen, and women, is a terrible index of the state of our civilization. "Atrocities are no less atrocities," said George Bernard Shaw, "when they occur in laboratories and are called medical research."

These abuses will not go away of themselves. Though they are medieval in spirit and practice, they are deeply entrenched and many of them are highly profitable to the multi-billion dollar laboratory animal and equipment industry and to other special interest groups. The tragedy of it lies also in the fact that there are other, newer methods of drug testing that are available which are

94

both cheaper and more reliable than animal testing, and all of which inflict no pain on any living creature. These include computer analysis, gas chromotography, and human tissue culture, among others.

Like the institution of slavery, or the practice of child abuse or wife abuse, or any other form of oppression of those who are defenseless, evils such as these need strong voices to be raised in protest, and vigorous actions to be taken, at the educational, the political, and the legal level.

To be a true New Age person it is not enough, in my opinion, to sign one's letters: "Love and Light!" It is not enough to Realize One's Full Potential through affirmations, visualization, decrees, mantras, meditation, group work, and prayer. To be a true New Age person, I believe, one needs to have a unitive consciousness—a sense of the unity with all that lives. And it inevitably follows that one must then live a life of genuine *ahimsa* or harmlessness to all living creatures, and helpfulness to all living creatures.

This means to be mindful of what one eats and what one wears. (As Dr. Dolittle put it, "When you dress in suede or leather, Or some fancy fur or feather, Do you stop and wonder whether for a fad You have killed some beast or other And you're wearing someone's brother or perhaps someone's mother?")

It means to be mindful of what products one uses, or refuses to use, and what medical research one contributes to or *refuses to contribute to.*

In short, to be a New Age person means not only to express concern, but to *show* concern, through all one's actions, for other beings, and especially for those other categories of life who cannot speak for themselves.

If you wish to express your concern for animals, here is a short list of excellent organizations of which you can become a member.

Beauty Without Cruelty, 175 W. 12th St., New York City, 10011

The Hermitage Animal Refuge (Sister Seraphim), 5278 E. 21st St., Tucson, Ariz. 85711

New England Anti-Vivisection Society, 9 Park St., Boston, Mass, 02108

Society for Animal Rights, 421 State St., Clark Summit, Pa. 18411

Animal Protection Institute of America (A.P.I.), 5894 Land Park Drive, P.O. Box 22505, Sacramento, Cal. 98522

Compassion in World Farming, 20 Lavant St., Petersfield, Hants, England

THE NATURAL CAT and THE FUR PERSON: Two Book Reviews

Hugh Lynn Cayce, for many years the managing director of the Association for Research and Enlightenment, was a very dedicated, energetic, talented, and kindly man. In addition, he had the endearing qualities of a sense of fun and a sense of humor.

One day when we were having lunch in Palo Alto, he invited me to lecture at an upcoming conference of the Association at Asilomar, near Carmel. I expressed reluctance to accept because I was busy with a number of things; and he began, in his persuasive way, to remind me how beautiful Asilomar was, and how delightful it was to see the deer and the raccoons that freely roamed the conference grounds. Jokingly I said that, much as I loved to see deer and raccoons, I really didn't like to go any place where there were no cats.

"That's no problem!" he said promptly. "Will you come if we import a cat? Or better still, if I have a cat introduce you to the audience?" Taken off guard, I said, "Well, yes, that might be an interesting experience." "Good! It's a deal," he said, extending his hand. "I'll tell the program committee you'll be there."

I shook hands laughing, feeling that I had let myself be conned into a lecture on the strength of a bit of banter, but not minding too much because Asilomar is a beautiful place, and after all, only two hours by car from Los Altos, where I was living at the time.

He really lived up to the bargain, however. Somehow he managed to draft a local cat into service. On the night of my lecture he went up on the platform, the cat in his arms, and proceeded to introduce me, rather flatteringly, as if the cat were talking. I was both touched and amused, and it all came off very well, especially since the cat he was fortunate enough to find was docile and well-behaved and sat with great aplomb in his arms as if knowing exactly what was being said.

I don't think I have much else in common with the French writer, Colette, but at least, like her, I seem to be synonymous in certain circles with cats. So it was inevitable, I suppose, that I was invited to do a review for the A.R.E. Journal *on* The Natural Cat. *It appeared in the November 1981 issue.*

*To me the book was significant on many counts, one of them being its emphasis on good nutrition for cats (*not canned cat food, with all its artificial flavors and colors, its additives and preservatives). *It also exemplified what I feel to be a newly emerging attitude toward animals—one in which they are valued for their* friendship, *rather than for their fur or their flesh.*

Gurdjieff once said: "One of the best ways of learning how to love is to learn to love an animal"—a statement which at first glance might seem strange or even demeaning to some people, but which in my opinion is very valid. Dr. Pitcairn, the veterinarian who wrote the introduction to The Natural Cat, *expressed the same idea in other terms; and the spirit of friendship and love is reflected beautifully on all the pages of this book.*

A few years after the unusual experience of being introduced to a lecture audience by a cat, I was living in Virginia Beach, and was invited by the editor of the SPCA Newsletter to write a book review for the forthcoming issue. I chose The Fur Person *by May Sarton as the one to review. It was not a new book—in fact, it first appeared in 1957—but it had just been reprinted in paperback. My enthusiasm for the book and my desire to see it remain in print and delight a wider circle of readers prompted the choice.*

The story of the little cat is written with great simplicity and charm; and its message, reflected in the title, is one which is emerging in many places. An animal is not to be regarded as a thing, and therefore treated with indifference to its feelings or exploited with callous cruelty. An animal is a sentient, sensitive, living being, as much a creation of God as we are; and to deny it personhood or even a soul is a theological bias to which I cannot subscribe. Only on one point do I disagree with the author. She concludes the book by saying: "A gentleman cat becomes a person when it is truly loved by a human being." The proposition may or may not hinge upon a purely semantic issue; but I am inclined to think that a cat—or any living being—is a person whether a human being loves him or not. If this be heresy, then call me heretic.

The Natural Cat: A Holistic Guide for Finicky Owners, *by Anitra Frazier with Norma Eckroate, Harbor Publishing, Inc. San Francisco, Calif., 1981. 200 pp. $7.95 paperback.*

The ancient Egyptians loved cats and, at certain periods, even worshiped them as a symbol of divinity. It was considered a serious crime to harm any member of the species; and when a beloved cat died, members of the family shaved their eyebrows as a sign of mourning.

The passionate cat lovers among us (and our number seems to be increasing) may well have been Egyptians once, in a far distant incarnation. For us, other animals may have charm, intelligence, and beauty; but none can inspire the fascination we feel, or the devotion, for the beauty, charm, and intelligence of the cat. For us, too, it is important that cats be treated with the respect and care that they deserve; and so it is exciting to come upon a recent book called *The Natural Cat: A Holistic Guide for Finicky Owners.*

Anitra Frazier—with the literary help of Norma Eckroate—composed the book. Her qualifications are impressive: She is New York City's only out-call cat groomer, and for the past eight years has worked in close cooperation with veterinarians and a feline behaviorist to help the cats she is called upon to serve. But in addition to this professional merit, she has a deep love for cats; and the love shines through on every page.

The topics covered are, in a way, no different from those covered in many other books on cat care: grooming, diet, home care of sick cats, going to the vet, and various behavioral problems found in cat-to-cat and cat-to-human relationships. But this is the difference: Anitra Frazier is very aware of the importance of nutrition as both a preventive and a corrective force in a cat's health.

"Early in my search for a high quality food," she writes, "it became obvious to me that most cat food stocked on grocery shelves did not seem to have the primary purpose of building health. Most simply sustain life, at least for a moderate time, before it endangers the cat's health with chemical additives, imbalances, and/or general low quality. Ingredients such as tuna and artificial flavors and scents tend to attract the cats and 'hook' them...Artificial flavors and colors are not food but chemicals that undermine health." She gives detailed suggestions for a high quality diet, including whole grains; raw and cooked vegetables; and meat, tofu, cheese, eggs, yogurt, and other proteins. Perhaps her most appealing addition to the feline diet is the Vita-Mineral Mix, an easy-to-prepare supplement of nutrients any cat will love.

These suggestions come as a welcome and exciting surprise to those of us who are aware of the fact that we are what we eat, and that there is an inescapable relationship between processed food and the degenerative diseases that are increasing in both the human and the pet population. Furthermore, as Edgar Cayce repeatedly suggests, we are what we eat and also what we *think.* And Anitra Frazier is aware of this, too. Her discussion of the psychological stresses to which cats are subject (including loud noises, absence of familiar people or being left alone, confinement or caging, lack of a hiding place, etc.) should be illuminating to people who have never thought seriously about the inner world of cats and how similar their psychological stresses can be to those that we experience.

In short, this is "a very special book," as Dr. Richard Pitcairn, veterinarian, states in his foreword. Dr. Pitcairn makes another statement that echoes this reviewer's sentiments exactly. He writes: "Many people have learned through relating to animals what it is to care for and accept responsibility for another being. All the basic elements of relationship are there—the same elements found in relationship with a friend, husband or wife, child, or even a plant. If one can discover how to relate fully to an animal, without exploitation, with real care and concern for its welfare and continued physical and psychological well-being, then one can relate to anyone. The skills involved are universal."

The Natural Cat may not be of interest to people who have little or no fondness for cats. But to those who do, it can serve not only as an excellent handbook for the care of cats, but also as a handbook for learning the universal skills needed in all relationships.

Those who love cats should be alerted to the fact that May Sarton's little classic, *The Fur Person,* is back in print again—this time only in paperback, alas.

The Fur Person, for those who may never have heard of it, concerns a little cat with a glossy tiger coat, a white shirt front, white paws, and a white tip on his tail who was successfully living the life of a Cat About Town, but finally wearied of the uncertainty of things and wanted to find a home of his very own. So he set about systematically to find a suitable one. After one unfortunate mistaken choice from which he managed to escape, he came upon two kindly spinster ladies with a house and a garden and a pear tree that admirably suited his needs. Brusque Voice and Gentle Voice, as he came to think of them, had impeccable taste, and knew better than to smother a self-respecting cat with too much attention. They also were marvellous cooks, and the haddock with cream they prepared as a first meal was heavenly. So, grateful for his good fortune, the Cat About Town decided to stay, and they gave him the name of Tom Jones.

Whenever Tom Jones became depressed or disturbed about anything he would do his yoga meditation. He observed all the Ten Commandments of the Gentleman Cat, such as: I. A Gentleman Cat has an immaculate shirt front and paws at all times. II. A Gentleman Cat allows no constraint of his person, even loving constraint...IX. A Gentleman Cat gives thanks after a Worthy Meal, by licking the plate so clean that a person might think it had been washed.

After coming home from the hospital, where a strange operation was performed, Tom Jones not only became more home-loving and peaceable than he had ever been before, but also came down with a bad cough and began to lose all his hair. It was horribly humiliating and depressing, and he began to fear that Gentle Voice and Brusque Voice wouldn't want him any more. But they gave him much loving care, applied a disgusting bottle of something to his hair, and before long his coat was shining and thick and beautiful again. It was then that he came to realize that they loved him not only for his handsome appearance, but for himself alone. They were not only housekeepers, but truly friends, who would not abandon him.

And so it was that he came to understand that he was not just a cat, but a Fur Person. "For a Fur Person is a cat whom human beings love in the right way, allowing him to keep his dignity, his reserve, and his freedom. And a Fur Person is a cat who has come to love one, or in very exceptional cases, two human beings, and who has decided to stay with them as long as he lives."

The Fur Person is a delightful experience, written with gentleness and insight. And, if you should find that it ends too soon, you can do as this reviewer did: start from the beginning and read it over again. Twice.

ANIMAL REGISTRY

Lord Dowding was the Chief Marshal of the Air Force in England during World War II, and was well known in his country for distinguished military service. After his retirement from the Air Force he wrote a clear, outspoken, carefully reasoned book about his experiences with spirit communication, which he entitled Many Mansions.

When I wrote my first book on the Cayce data on reincarnation, and called it Many Mansions, *I was unaware of the existence of Lord Dowding's book; but no lawsuit resulted and no harm was done; titles are not copyrighted.*

Lord Dowding's second wife was a beautiful woman, a dancing teacher named Muriel Whiting, who felt that she had a special mission in the world—to help the animal kingdom. In 1959 she founded an organization which she called Beauty Without Cruelty, dedicated primarily to making people aware of the cruelties involved in the cosmetics and the fur industries, and aware also of the fact that cruelty-free alternatives are becoming more and more available. The organization now has an animal sanctuary in Sussex, England, and has branches in Australia, New Zealand, Canada, Scotland, Japan, Rhodesia, and the United States.

It also has a journal called Compassion, *and it was in the winter 1967 issue of this magazine that the following article of mine was published.*

*I personally find it of interest that Muriel Dowding's mother was a Theosophist, as was my mother, and that Muriel Dowding herself became very active in the Theosophical Society in later years. She relates in her autobiography (*The Psychic Life of Muriel, the Lady Downing*), that she and her husband were in communication with invisible intelligences who encouraged them and guided them in the work of assisting the animal kingdom.*

It is interesting to note a parallel here with Findhorn, that remarkable community where flowers and vegetables flourish in a cold, sandy, windswept spot of northern Scotland where such vegetation has never

101

flourished before. It is claimed by Peter and Eileen Caddy, the founders of Findhorn, that Findhorn could not have existed were it not for the guidance they received from invisible intelligences, who communicated through the sensitivity of Dorothy Maclean and Eileen Caddy.*

The effort to help lost and homeless animals described in the following article is certainly a minor enterprise compared to the effort to correct the vast crimes now being committed against animals all over the world. But minor though it may be, it is none the less an important and much-needed expression of concern, and one which could well be imitated elsewhere.

In Menlo Park, California—a small community about thirty-five miles south of San Francisco—there exists a unique service for animals and people known as the Animal Registry.

Founded two years ago by an Englishwoman, Miss Jean Miller, and her friend, Mrs. Alice Hodges, the Animal Registry is a volunteer service carried on almost completely by telephone, with the purpose of reuniting lost pets with their owners.

As a visitor in Miss Miller's library one afternoon, I had the interesting experience of seeing how the service works.

The phone rings. Miss Miller answers it, opens a stenographer's notebook marked CATS on the cover and turns to the column marked FOUND. As she talks to the caller, she makes notations in the notebook. "Small tiger cat, female, short-haired, found Monday evening, around 7 p.m., vicinity of San Antonio Road and Portola Drive in Los Altos. Friendly; very hungry." She adds the name, address, and phone number of the person who made the call; asks if she (the finder) could shelter the cat a few days; and promises to inform her promptly if anyone calls who has lost a cat answering this description.

In the hour or so that I sat there, there were some eleven phone calls—some regarding dogs (who are listed in a separate notebook) and some regarding cats. Ducks, rabbits, birds, and turtles are also included in the service, but these of course are not so frequently called about. Every day brings from five to thirty phone calls.

Miss Miller—who earns her living by running two poodle grooming shops, but who spends most of her time working on the Animal Registry—is a blonde, attractive woman, of English and Scotch descent, with clear blue eyes and a very pleasant, patient manner.

She sees her function to be that of bringing together a

---

*See *The Magic of Findhorn,* by Paul Hawken (Harper & Row, 1975) and *The Findhorn Garden,* by the Findhorn Community, with a foreword by Wm. Erwin Thompson (Harper & Row, 1975)

distraught owner of a lost pet with the finder of it—a function which city pounds are too overcrowded and understaffed to perform; but she also sees herself as an educator as well. Much of her time on the phone is spent advising people what procedures to follow in trying to locate a pet, or in educating them in humane attitudes and behavior. "It is surprising to discover how little people know about the needs of a helpless animal," she said. "Dogs and cats have collapsed from hunger and people have not fed them because they 'didn't want to encourage them,' as they say. The need for humane education is great."

Animal Registry has some fascinating case histories to its credit.

One is that of a beautiful, black, yellow-eyed Persian cat, which was carried by its young owner in the annual spring Pet Parade in Palo Alto—a small university community which borders the town of Menlo Park. The cat was frightened by a dog, and, escaping its basket, disappeared into the crowd.

The child and his parents were frantic, as they loved the cat dearly; but they were especially concerned because the cat had been declawed, and consequently could not easily hunt for food or defend itself. Desperately, they ran ads in several local papers, visited the various pounds and shelters daily, and—fortunately—listed their name and phone number and the cat's description with the Animal Registry. This was in May of 1966.

Three months later, in the middle of August, an elderly lady phoned concerning a very thin black cat with long matted hair and yellow eyes which she had been feeding, but which she had decided to take to the pound. Miss Miller checked back through all the cats in her LOST columns and came upon her notation of the previous May. Could this be the same cat?

The people who had lost the black cat were away on a trip; so Mrs. Hodges kept the bedraggled waif in her home for three weeks until their return. Then a visit of inspection established the fact that it was, indeed, the same cat! and a happy homecoming ensued.

Cats and dogs which have been lost for as long as seven and one-half months have been reunited with their owners through this service.

Frequently the Registry is able to find a home for a lost animal that is reported to them, not with its former owner, but with someone else; and much of Miss Miller's time is spent in rescue work of various kinds. Mrs. Hodges, who specializes in cats, while Miss Miller's special interest is dogs, makes daily rounds feeding wild cats who take shelter in an old abandoned building near the railway station.

How do people know about the service? Miss Miller runs a small ad in the PETS column of several newspapers (there are several communities clustered together in this area). The ad simply advises people to check with Animal Registry, if they lose or find an animal, and gives the phone number of Miss Miller, Mrs. Hodges, and of whatever assistant they may happen to have.

No charge is made for this service, though the phone bills and the cost of advertising is considerable every month. It is a work of pure dedication and love on the part of Miss Miller and Mrs. Hodges.

Miss Miller—who has a pilot's license and who drove for the Fire Brigade in London in World War II—is deeply concerned about all aspects of animal welfare. Though, when founding Animal Registry, she was trying merely to meet what she felt was an urgent local need, she agreed that a service of this kind could be established in many communities, all over the world.

Persons who are physically handicapped, or retired persons who do not wish to leave their homes and yet wish to be useful, could perform a great service to pets and people by starting an Animal Registry of their own. Or they need be neither handicapped nor retired, but merely interested—and concerned. A small fee (say 50¢) for a pet that has been restored to its owner might serve to cover the telephone and advertising charges in the case of persons doing the service who could not afford such an outlay of money.

Until such time as pets learn not to wander—or until such time as they can be summoned and guided home by telepathic messages!—a clearing house of this kind will remain a much-needed and a much-appreciated service in this world.

LET'S HAVE HOLISTIC ANIMAL LOVERS

There are many memorable literary passages and many acutely perceptive insights in the work of Somerset Maugham. Among these—for me—is a passage in his book The Summing Up. *He wrote:*

I think what has chiefly struck me in human beings is their lack of consistency. I have never seen people all of a piece. I have often asked myself how characteristics, seemingly irreconcilable, can exist in the same person. I have known crooks who were capable of self-sacrifice, sneak thieves who were sweet-natured, and harlots for whom it was a point of honor to give good value for money.

Again, in The Moon and Sixpence, *he made a similar observation:*

I think I was a little disappointed in her. I expected then people to be more of a piece than I do now, and I was distressed to find so much vindictiveness in so charming a creature. I did not realize how motley are the qualities that go to make up a human being. Now I am well aware that pettiness and grandeur, malice and charity, hatred and love, can find place side by side in the same human heart.

Maugham in these two passages expressed an observation which I later found confirmed and illustrated hundreds of times.

The following piece is in a sense a commentary on the same theme, though the inconsistency involved in the case of animal lovers is perhaps less one of character than of something else. To be more precise: I have seen a group of animal lovers go to a corner restaurant, after their animal welfare meeting is over, to get a snack. They continue their discussion, voicing their passionate concern about some ordinance affecting dogs and cat, all the while eating a ham sandwich . . . It is virtually certain that not a single one of them would deliberately go out and treat a pig cruelly; yet their eating of the ham sandwich represents either a total ignorance or total insensitivity to the manner in which ham and all pork products are now produced.

The attitude of the meat producers is well summed up in Singer and Mason's Animal Factories *in quoting the Walls Meat Company: "The* *breeding sow would be thought of, and treated as, a valuable piece of machinery whose function it is to pump out baby pigs like a sausage machine." The total immobility in which female pigs are kept during the gestation period and again when nursing the piglets should cause any thoughtful person who knows the misery of confinement to give serious thought to the whole matter.**

So the contradiction to which I am referring here is probably less a contradiction in basic character, but rather a curious inconsistency that probably principally involves lack of information. Or, where information concerning the cruelties of pig raising are even dimly known about, there arises a conflict with the inertia of custom and lifelong habit.

Having read Maugham, I think I have become less judgmental of such inconsistencies—especially since I can observe a few within myself!—but none the less I think it is salutory to point them out—which is the reason for the following article.

Many of us have come to realize that if we wish health, we must seek it holistically. It is my strong feeling that, if we wish to call ourselves animal lovers, we should love them not fragmentarily, but holistically. And if we find it impossible to live without a ham sandwich, the least, in all decency, we can do, is to allow the little pig the dignity and comfort of a relatively normal life.

Not long ago I received an invitation to a banquet from the local Audubon Society. The Audubon Society, in case anybody does not happen to be familar with it, was named after John James Audubon, a nineteenth-century ornithologist whose book, *The Birds of America,* is still regarded as a classic. It contains 1,065 pictures of some 489 different species of birds, all painstakingly rendered by Audubon himself. The Society was founded in 1905, has approximately 400,000 members in the United States, and was originally dedicated to the protection of wild birds and animals. Since 1935 its scope has broadened somewhat to include other conservation causes, but its emphasis is still upon birds and their protection.

The invitation that I received from the Society stated that they were planning to serve roast chicken at their annual banquet. Be it said to their credit that they were not planning to serve four and twenty blackbirds, baked in a pie; or roast pheasant under glass; or fricassee of bald eagle or some other exotic or endangered species. And, I grant you, a chicken is probably not usually classified as one of the wild birds whom the Audubonians vow to protect. None the less, a chicken *is* a bird; and I don't quite

*A six-hour bus trip in a Greyhound bus, a forty-seven-hour flight on an excursion trip to India, or a four-week stay in a hospital bed with a broken leg should serve to give some insight into the misery and frustration of confinement. Imagine it to be life-long. . . .

understand what logic exists that makes it possible to assemble devotedly to discuss the protection of certain kinds of birds while placidly eating the body of another. Somehow I have the same sense of strange discrepancy that I would have if I had received an invitation from the National Cat Protection Society inviting me to a banquet where they were scheduling a dinner of roast cat.

A few months later I received another invitation from a nearby Society for the Prevention of Cruelty to Animals, requesting reservations for their annual banquet, and an indication of which entree one preferred: roast chicken or veal parmigiana. I attended the banquet, but I could not help noticing that I was the only person present who had ordered an entree (salad, baked potato, and cottage cheese) which was not on the menu and which was not the result of the most appalling cruelty to farm animals. The good people of the Society talked a great length that evening about their accomplishments of the past year and their projects for the coming year regarding local cats and dogs—a cause with which I am in deepest sympathy. But nobody seemed to be even slightly aware of, or concerned about, the horrifying things that are being routinely done to chickens and veal calves all over the country in what is known (euphemistically and deceptively) as "intensive farming."

In both the Audubon Society and the Society for the Prevention of Cruelty to Animals, the membership could hardly be said to consist of brutal people or insensitive clods. On the contrary: the members are almost invariably sensitive to other life forms and altruistically concerned about their protection. But they are, for the most part—like the rest of the population—woefully ignorant concerning the sources of our food supply, and willfully kept so by advertisers paid by agribusinessmen to make us believe, with charming and whimsical pictures, that pigs dance gaily to slaughter and that eggs are idyllically produced on "farms" by happily cackling hens.

In reality, farms as we once knew them are rapidly disappearing, and vast buildings in which animals are confined in small cages, stalls, and pens for their entire lifetimes are taking their place. The confinement system is designed for convenience, maximum productivity, and profit. No concern is shown for the physical and psychological well-being of the animals. Neither chickens nor pigs nor veal calves have even the minimal pleasure of sunshine or movement. Especially in the case of the chickens, they are so crowded together in small cages that unsanitary and disease-inviting conditions are prevalent. To deal with the diseases, sulfa drugs, antibiotics, pesticides, disinfectants, and other chemicals are in constant use; and the stressful conditions also require that tranquilizers be administered, and the chickens' beaks burned or cut off so that they do not injure each other in their frustration. Hormones are also often given to promote rapid growth. Common sense should tell us that such a battery of powerful chemicals can hardly result in meat or eggs that are conducive to human health.*

I suppose I should not become impatient with the good people of the Audubon Society and the SPCA. They are all doing a very good job, with small resources and very little encouragement from the establishment. I must remind myself that all of us are inconsistent in the practice of our ideals; that none of us can be informed about everything; and that—as Lady Muriel Dowding once told me over the luncheon table in London—it is better to be inconsistently kind than consistently cruel.

But at the same time, I am hoping that before too many years have passed, when I receive another invitation to a banquet given by the Audubon Society and the SPCA, their menu plans will be different. I am hoping that instead of serving the cooked corpses of pathetically confined chickens and veal calves they will be offering a choice of nut loaf, tofu roast, or soybean patties instead.

Or, if they simply cannot give up the meat they are accustomed to since childhood, I hope they will begin to work, with as much dedication as they give to birds, cats, and dogs, for the liberation of food animals from their abnormal slavery. If one insists on eating meat, the very least one can do in good conscience is to guarantee to the animals that one eats some semblance of a *life,* not a living death, before they go to slaughter.

---

*For further information about the conditions which animals endure, write to Action for Life, Box 5888, Washington, D.C. 20014; Friends of Animals, 11 West 60th Street, NYC 10023 and Compassion in World Farming, 20 Lavant Street, Petersfield, Hants, England. Also read Peter Singer's two books, *Animal Liberation* and (with Jim Mason) *Animal Factories.*

DISNEYLAND FOR CATS

One of the many advantages of being a lecturer is that one gets to visit many cities one might otherwise not think of visiting. Though I was living in Los Altos, California, at the time I wrote this article, I might not have gone to Sacramento unless I had been invited there to speak.

While in Sacramento, I happened to hear of Mrs. Avellino's unusual project, and, always interested in anything that affects the welfare of cats, I made a point of visiting her place. I was greatly impressed by it, not merely because of its colorful inventiveness, but largely because of the solution it offered to the problem of cats in cities who wander, and disappear—the victims of street accidents, theft, and assorted cruelties.

Cinderland, as Mrs. Avellino called it, became a real educational center. Unfortunately vandalism became prevalent in the neighborhood, and the Avellinos moved to a mountainous area, far from town, and dissassembled the wonderland they had created.

Like the Animal Registry described in a preceding article, Cinderland represents a very minor contribution to the many problems that animals face. But it is a valuable example of the humble ways in which concerned people can express their love for animals, and a valuable model for others to follow.

The article was published in Peninsula Living *in the weekend of July 20/21 edition, 1968.*

Human beings have their Disneyland. It seems only fair, therefore, that cats should have their own fantasy playground—a place called Cinderland.

It all started four years ago when a tiny little all-black kitten turned up on the front porch of Mr. and Mrs. Aldo Avellino's home in suburban Sacramento. He was scrawny and pathetic and hungry and scared, and the Avellinos—who had never had a cat before—decided to take him in. They called him Cinder.

What Cinder didn't know—and what the Avellinos didn't know, either—was that four years later they'd be featured on a coast-to-coast television special about cats. "Big Cats, Little Cats," a well-received documentary, ran last spring. The reason for all this exposure: a wonderland for cats, named in honor of Cinder, which the Avellinos created little by little for the black kitten and for the other five stray cats they eventually adopted.

Basically, Cinderland is a 40 by 60-foot enclosure, six feet high, made with boards and chicken wire on four sides and on top. It comprises approximately half of the entire back yard of the Avellino home. Its original purpose was to provide a way of letting little Cinder enjoy the sunshine, grass, and fresh air out-of-doors, without running the risk of getting lost or being killed by cars on the two busy streets which border the Avellino corner lot.

Key to the Avellinos' project was the appearance on the market of a specially-constructed flexible cat-door. When placed in a door or wall of the house, this device allows a cat to go in and out without disturbing the owners, and without allowing the entry of flies.

The Avellinos installed this door in one of their bedrooms, and enclosed a large expanse of lawn outside with chicken wire. This was the beginning.

From this simple start, an incredible fairyland evolved. It was characterized, as is the Anaheim version for humans, by color, imagination, humor, and charm.

There is a Cat-Nap Hotel, a fish pond and water fall; a Space Ship ("Beat Those Russian Cats Or Bust!"); a covered wagon; an eight-car train; 26 houses Cinderland Village; a palace; a catnip garden; a fountain; a candy mint-colored patio; a royal carriage (a pink baby carriage pulled by a stuffed pink poodle); carpeted stairways and tunnels; a variety of catnip toys to play with; and many other colorful and imaginative creations, in which or with which cats may amuse themselves and in turn, amuse people.

And people do come to see Cinderland, literally by the thousands. The Humane Society of the United States, California Branch, endorses it for its humane education values; and a small sign reading "H.S.U.S.—Cinderland" is on the back gate. But this is its only marker. Cinderland has never been advertised, and no one would suspect its existence behind the neat residence in the quiet neighborhood where the Avellinos live. Yet its fame has spread all over the country.

110

But Cinderland is not merely an amazing spectacle, unique of its kind in the world. It serves—and was intended, almost from the start, to serve—an educational purpose, also. Mrs. Avellino is a woman with a flair for decorating. Her husband shares her love for pets and enjoys implementing her ideas with construction.

The basic idea with which the Avellinos started was controlled outdoor freedom—especially for cats; since cats, unlike dogs, can so easily climb trees and fences and hence escape from an ordinary fenced back yard.

"A cat or dog allowed to roam the streets in cities and suburbs today is alive only by accident," Mrs. Avellino says. And while all persons might not have the time or inclination to create another Cinderland, almost any person can construct, or have constructed for him, a simple outdoor enclosure which keeps the pet both safe and happy.

The inspiration which Cinderland already has given to people is a matter of record. Mrs. Avellino has a file containing letters from scores of visitors throughout the country. The writers visited Cinderland, returned home and built a similar, if more modest, playground for their own pets. And these are only the persons who have taken the trouble to write to her, sometimes enclosing photographs.

A dramatic example of this is seen in the case of a man whose neighbors had for months been complaining to the police and to humane authorities about the continuous barking of his three large German shepherd dogs. He kept the dogs in a small enclosure in his back yard, filled with garbage, litter, and lumber. There was no room to run in. One day he noticed the Cinderland sign, and a troop of children entering. Curious, he asked if he might come in also. Apparently what he saw there made him ashamed of his own neglect. Within a few days he had cleaned up the space where his dogs were kept and used the lumber to enlarge it. He even decorated it, somewhat, on the model of Cinderland. The neighbors don't complain any more, because the dogs no longer bark fretfully in a space too small and dirty for comfort.

Mrs. Avellino, however, not only advocates controlled outdoor freedom for pets and improved standards for pet care.She also advocates kindness to all living creatures, and uses the frequent visits of children and adults as opportunities to put her point across. She has passed out more than 30,000 pieces of literature on the subject, especially on the importance of spaying cats and dogs to help cut the tragic and expensive overpopulation problem of animals.

Even before Sacramento TV stations featured Cinderland, Cinder—who started it all—had received thousands of letters from school children. This might be because he answers with a loud and distinct "Huh?" when his name is called.

The cats in Cinderland invite you to visit next time you're in Sacramento. Perhaps you'll be inspired to create a Cinderland in your own yard.

Your animal friends will be delighted.

ZSA ZSA GETS
A POODLE CUT

Zsa Zsa is one of my current coterie of cats, and for the last six years has both enriched my life with her beauty and tried my soul with her prima donna temperament.

She had been abandoned by her owners—a common occurrence everywhere, but especially so in a summer resort town like Virginia Beach— and someone found her and brought her in to the SPCA. I was doing volunteer work there at the time, several mornings a week. and I was captivated by her loveliness, which could have graced any calendar of cats with distinction. So I took her home with me. She was very pregnant at the time.

Shortly after I adopted her she came into my study late one night, and told me very insistently, in an unusual tone of voice and with back and fro movements from my desk to the door, that she wanted me to leave my desk and follow her. I followed her downstairs to the kitchen, where she went into a cupboard and proceeded very soon to give birth to six tiny kittens. I midwifed them all, from midnight to five A.M., but unfortunately all of them died within a few days, probably because of malnutrition during the early weeks of her pregnancy.

Zsa Zsa continues to be a beautiful creature, and seems to be well aware of the fact. The following account of her is totally factual.

I have a cat named Zsa Zsa.

She is a gorgeous long-haired cat, of an ethereal color somewhere between cream and very pale apricot; but honesty compels the admission that she is not the sweetest cat ever invented. She has the bad habit of whining at the dinner table for tidbits (I have a friend who is thinking of writing a piece about her called "Whining and Dining with Zsa Zsa"); and she never tolerates more than one minute of petting before she growls angry disapproval and leaps off my lap.

Worst of all, she absolutely refuses to let me comb anything but the long, lovely hair around her head. To attempt to go any further is to risk hideous hisses, a demonic expression that would strike terror in the breast of Count Dracula, and assorted claw wounds. Of all the cats I've ever had (and I have had a goodly number), Zsa Zsa is the only one I have ever been afraid of.

The result: Zsa Zsa goes about with snarls and mats in her hair, and fastidious visitors look at me as if I were an unfit mother.

Things had come to a very unpretty pass this past May. Zsa Zsa's coat looked like a flat, bulgy, badly made hooked rug; and just one too many people had said to me, with strained politeness, "Don't you ever comb her *hair*?"

So I decided to take her to a professional groomer. I felt it only fair to tell the proprietor, when I phoned, that Zsa Zsa was difficult. "Oh, we never have any problems with cats," she said, cheerily.

I liked her self-assurance, but wondered none the less whether she carried adequate life and accident insurance. "Is there a clause in your policy—ah—covering claw wounds...?" I started to say, but thought better of it.

Finally, after two days of brooding over the possibility of being sued if Zsa Zsa inflicted bodily injury, I decided to risk it and I took her to be bathed and groomed.

When I went to pick her up five hours later, I was relieved, first of all, to see that the salon was quietly humming with normal activity; and all of the attendants seemed quite unharmed.

"Did you have any trouble with her?" I asked hesitantly, as I paid the bill.

"None at all," the groomer said, rather curtly, I thought, as if professionally offended. I found it hard to believe, but the woman seemed rushed and I didn't press the point. Since Zsa Zsa was crouched in the very depths of a large and rather dark cat carrier, I did not get a full view of anything but two baleful green eyes until I got her home and opened the door of the carrier.

Timidly she stepped out into the living room. And what a sight I beheld! A cat with a poodle cut!!

The hair around her head was as long and beautiful as before. And the magnificence of her bushy tail had not been touched. But, except for her legs, the rest of her body was sleek, svelte, covered only with shortly cropped silky hair. For the first time in her life I could see the lithe and elegant lines of her little cat body, up till

114

now always hidden beneath that tremendous mass of hair. It was as if, having always seen a pretty girl swaddled in heavy Eskimo coats, I now could see her in a form-hugging body stocking. As for her legs, the groomer had, with real artistry, made it appear that, in front, she was wearing long, high-fashion fur gloves, reaching just over the elbows, and in back, sporting expensive and very chic fur boots. In short, she looked absolutely smashing.

I called the groomer to let her know how pleased I was. "She'll be much cooler during the summer months ahead," the woman said. "In fact," she went on, expansively, "we have a regular client, an English lady, who has her two long-haired cats clipped like that every spring so they won't suffer from the heat. Besides, with body hair so short you won't be as likely to have a flea problem with her, either. And she won't swallow so much hair when she washes herself, and get a lot of hair balls."

Still wondering if they had anesthetized Zsa Zsa, hypnotized her, whipped her, or restrained her in irons, I repeated my question of before. "You really didn't have any trouble with her?"

"Not at all," she repeated.

Marveling, and feeling less of a competent cat-lover than I always thought I was, I let it go at that. I console myself with the thought that even terrible-tempered cats can become docile in alien territory. And I fantasize that maybe—with a little publicity—Zsa Zsa could set a comfortable and elegant summer fashion for other long-haired cats.

In fact, I can see a whole new vista opening for the grooming parlors. "Be a Cool Cat!" the TV commercial could go. "I love my new summer outfit," the beautiful cat model could purr, sensuously, as she sashayed down the runway, waving her feathery plume of a tail.

Thanks to Zsa Zsa—bless her crabby little heart*—things in Catland might never be the same again.

---

*Interesting footnote. Actually, since coming home from the groomer, Zsa Zsa's temperament has improved. She still whines at the dinner table; but she now sits in my lap without temper outbursts, for long periods of time, and lets me pet her as much as I wish. Maybe they *did* put her in irons, after all, and she appreciates me more than she ever did before. I'll probably never know.

PART V:
FOR THE FUN OF IT

Voltaire once said: "If I had a son who wanted to be a writer, I think I would take him to the River Seine and drown him out of sheer parental affection."

Voltaire was jesting, of course, but I can understand why he made so dark a jest. Writing is hard work—far harder, both physically and mentally, than the average person imagines. At the same time it can be fun. It gives one a great sense of satisfaction to see one's thoughts take shape in a form that can shift people's perspective regarding life's perplexities, or that can stir them to action or to laughter.

The following five pieces are quite dissimilar in subject matter; their common denominator is that they were written in a spirit of fun and in the hope of making someone laugh.

HOW I GO ON A FAST

I was probably nineteen or twenty when I wrote the following piece. The reference to a brother is purely apocryphal. I don't have a brother. The allusion to eating stew is purely literary. At the time I had already become a vegetarian and wasn't eating stew, though I might still have been tempted, somewhat, by its aroma. The rest of the article, though slightly exaggerated, is essentially a faithful account of the difficulties I experienced, and I'm sure others experience, in trying to stay on a fast. As Emile Coue points out, when there is a struggle between the imagination and the will, the imagination always wins.

I still believe strongly in the benefits of fasting and go on fasts periodically, sometimes one day a week, sometimes for a period of three or four days. The longest one I ever managed was six and a half days.

There is another kind of fast that I read about somewhere which is equally beneficial, I think, on an ego level, and that is to fast for one day at least, or more if possible, from all criticism, of anyone or anything. I would like, cordially, to recommend it to the reader, beginning as of now.

I had just been re-reading Upton Sinclair's classic, *The Fasting Cure,* and an article in a recent health magazine called "Fasting—The Fountain of Eternal Youth." The result was that I decided to to on a fast.

"I am going on a fast," I announced to my family, as I drank a cup of hot water at the breakfast table.

"What would you like to have in the refrigerator in case you change your mind?" asked my mother.

I resented this allusion to my past fasts and replied, haughtily, "I have no intention of eating anything for the next seven days."

"What are you going to do, eat at night?" interposed my brother, irreverently.

I treated this remark with the complete disregard it deserved.

"Fasting," I continued, addressing the more intelligent portion of the family, "increases the metabolism and purifies the blood stream."

"Well, I'll have some fresh celery cabbage for you and make some mayonnaise, just in case you change your mind," reiterated my mother.

"That won't be necessary," I said, coldly. I rose with dignity from the breakfast table, feeling a distinct sense of victory. I had tasted nothing but hot water. Visions of a perfect complexion and a superbly remolded physique passed through my mind, which already began to feel that sense of clearness and lightness which Upton Sinclair so well describes.

I passed the corner candy shoppe, on my way to work, with my usual self-congratulation that I had passed far beyond that form of human folly. But today I passed even the fruit and vegetable market with a delightful sense of superiority. I was beyond even the fruits and vegetables.

I took deep breaths of the vitality-charged air (my friends tell me that I sound like a steam-calliope when I do this; but is not Health the Supreme Good?) and quoted complacently to myself a line I once came across in Hamlet: "I eat the air, promise crammed."

Toward noon I began to sense communications from my department of the interior; and when Agnes said, "Aren't you coming to lunch?" I replied, "No—I ate such a big breakfast I'm not really hungry." After all, Jesus *did* say "Fast in secret"; and feeling like a twentieth-century saint I busied myself with other things and ate no lunch.

I arrived home about six and found myself thinking of celery cabbage and mayonnaise—my favorite salad. The family had already sat down to supper, since I had told them not to wait for me. They were eating stew. It smelled delicious.

I decided I had better remain in the living room. I turned on the radio and began to wonder what I was doing on a fast. My complexion wasn't bad and everybody told me I had a nice figure anyway. My metabolism probably wasn't bad, either. And why worry about Eternal Youth?

But after all, a vow was a vow. Especially when it was made in public, before one's family. I made up my mind then and there that the next time I decided to go on a fast I would tell nobody about it.

Then I could modify a hasty and ill-considered course of action without loss of prestige. I began to muse on how many marriages there would be if people didn't have to announce the engagement first, and then live with their error in judgment.

The family had finished eating by now and were deciding whether or not to go to the movies. "We'll never make the seven o'clock show if I wash the dishes," my mother was saying. "I'll wash them," I called out, like the little girl scout I was. But a moment afterward I realized my folly. I was a potential criminal, leading myself to the scene of a potential crime.

Well, the family was gone, now; the dishes were washed and dried—all except the fruit-juicer. Fatal circumstance! It occurred to me, as I dried it, that a bit of grapefruit juice would really be a very delightful sort of thing; and really quite harmless, too. Wasn't it in Johanna Brandt's "Grape Cure" that I read than when starting a fast, the first day or two one really *should* have a bit of grape juice, to make the transition more gradual? After all, a fast was a dangerous thing—Upton Sinclair said so himself—so did Hauser—and the first day, after all, one could have a bit of grapefruit juice. It was a wonderful alkalizer, too, and after all....

I drank some grapefruit juice.

I had to stay in that evening to get some letters written and to wait for a telephone call; and along about eight o'clock when the letters were off my mind I began to think of other things. Of the tangerines in the refrigerator principally.

They were lovely tangerines. There was such a pungent fragrance about them! Something that suggested Christmas trees, and something that suggested California, and vibrant, glorious health! Suddenly I recelled an article I had read about a "fruit fast" that some movie star recommended. One ate nothing but fruit for a week. The results were supposed to be nothing short of marvelous. And the wonderful thing about it was that it didn't weaken you. Come to think of it, I was feeling a bit weak. I thought of my heart. Suddenly I could feel it beat. Weakness was bad on the heart. Yes, really, I shouldn't be playing with life and death like this. I really owed it to myself and to my family to eat those tangerines. This would be a *fruit* fast. I would eat three tangerines today, some apples tomorrow....

Well, if it was to be a fruit fast I was anxious to start it right away. I went to the refrigerator. There were four tangerines. I ate them all. My appetite was fully roused by now, and I looked for some more tangerines. But there weren't any. There were no apples, either.

So I went back to the living room and turned on the radio. I found myself musing on what is the *real* difference between a "fruit" and a "vegetable." After all, a vegetable was *fruit* of the earth; and who was I to draw the line? Tomatoes, for example, could be well classified as either "vegetable" or "fruit." And celery cabbage, too. That juicy, tender sweetness—that lush white perfection—it really reminded one of fruit. In fact, it probably *was* a fruit, in more senses than one. And after all, it was a *natural* food, filled with nature's vitamins and minerals.

An hour later the family returned from the movies and found me in the kitchen eating celery cabbage.

"I saved you some of the stew," said my mother, casually, as she came in. "And there's a piece of strawberry shortcake too. Of course I don't know whether it will increase the metabolism or purify the blood stream, but if you'd like to have it. . . ."

This evidence of skepticism on my mother's part could have annoyed me, and would have annoyed me, three hours previous. But Armageddon had been fought and lost.

"Well," I said, "I've decided to postpone my fast till my vacation. It's much too—ah—weakening. Where's the stew?"

So this is how I went on my last fast. If my experiences can be of any interest to other earnest souls, seeking Glorious Health and Eternal Youth, here they are, for what they are worth. Personally, I am beginning to feel that the only way I can go on a seven-day fast is to emigrate to India during one of their severer years of famine.

SING YO HO HO!

There are certain rewards for teaching in high school which compensate for some of the difficulties. At least there were in the time when I taught Italian at Lincoln High School in Milwaukee, before the days of drugs and violence. One of these rewards is the wonderful gems of misinformation one gathers in class and on examination papers. (A few items from my collection: "What was the Sermon on the Mount?" "A sermon given on a horse." "Which gland most affects human growth?" "The pecuniary gland.") Another reward is being surrounded all day by students at the age of frisky young colts, who, for all their adolescent problems, are none the less usually filled with ebullient spirits and a sense of fun.

I grew very fond of many of my students, some of whom became lasting friends. On one occasion, with a particularly delightful group, I wrote a short poem about each member of the class. I still remember a few of them:

Peter and Richard read comic books as though they
    were paid to do so.
When they get married we'll have to put some comic
    books in their trousseau.

Joe Glorioso was a comfort,
Joe Glorioso was joy,
Joe Glorioso always knew the place,
A wonder, for a boy!

A pleasant smile, a dear little face,
In all her marks she takes first place.
Poems are made by fools like me,
But only God could make Marie.

Angie Caravella, like a little caramella
    was so sweet that you could eat her all at once!

She'd only be a bite, but in this I'm sure I'm right,
The boy who loves our Angie is no dunce!

The following longer poem (written in the style of Vachel Lindsay's The Congo) was prompted by my exasperation at my only partly successful efforts to correct the bad grammar and the bad nutritional habits (white flour! white sugar!) of several interesting boys who were inseparable out-of-school companions: Joe D'Amato, Joe Carini, Charlie Busalacchi, and Frank Corrao. The principal culprit was Joe D'Amato, whose grammar, punctuation, and tardy habits were especially horrendous at the time. My nickname among them was "Cermy" (pronounced Shermee) and though they kidded me mercilessly about being a vegetarian and for my other unorthodoxies, I think they felt the same affection for me that I felt for them.

SING YO, HO, HO!

(With Apologies to Vachel Lindsay)

I

Yo, ho, ho, and a bottle of beer!
Sing yo, heave, ho, for the gang's all here!
Joe Carini, with his elbows on the table,
And dear old Busie playing hard as he was able,
Hard as he was able on the piano in the room—
(Boomlay, boomlay, boomlay, boom!)
And Frank Corrao and his pal D'Amato,
Singing wicked ditties in a way they hadn't ought to.
Yo, ho, ho, and a case of bock beer!
Sing yo, heave, ho, for the gang's all here!

II

When all of a sudden, in a blinding flash
And an ear-splitting thunderous sulphurous crash
The DEVIL appeared! (May his tribe decrease)
And every least sound in the room did cease.
Cloaked in red satin and hooded in black,
His horns just showing and his tail in back,
He leaned on the piano in a pose debonair
(And Busie twitched slightly on the piano chair.)
His handsome dark face with its eyes of fire
Looked every bit as wicked as a copy of *Esquire*.

III

"Gentlemen," he bowed, "This is such a treat."
(Frank sank down in the nearest seat.)

"There has been," he continued, "a strike down in hell."
(Joe looked at Joe, and neither felt well.)
"And this most unfortunate state of affairs
Necessitates, gentlemen, my trip upstairs.
"When I heard you all Corraosing (and please forgive the pun)
I thought it only proper to interrupt such rowdy fun
And choose which one among you has the very blackest soul
To come on down with me to hell and help to stoke the coal."

IV

Joe Carini trembled and he thought of Lee.
Dear old Busie thought, "I hope it's not me!"
Corrao thought, "Lord, how I hate hot weather!"
D'Amato turned as pale as the whitest of heather.
"And in order to determine," the Devil then resumed,
"Who is the blackest sinner here (for nothing is assumed)
"I have a simple test with me. It takes the merest trice
For us to know with certainty who really isn't nice."
He took four toothpicks from his handsome sleeve of sable
And tossed them nonchalantly upon the parlor table.

V

"You each take one," he directed, suave as ever.
"And though it looks so simple, it really is quite clever.
The sticks are specially treated so that he who's black in soul
Will turn the stick within his hand to a black as black as coal."
Carini, sadly thinking of the white bread that he'd ate
Now wished he'd heeded Cermi before it was too late.
Corrao recalled, regretful, all the girls that he had kissed,
And Busie thought with guilt of all the practice he had missed.
D'Amato thought of nothing, but he turned as cold as ice.
And the Devil said, "Gentlemen, make your choice!"

VI

A deathly horrid silence hung (like California fog)
On the little scene enacted with the fragments of a log.
The sticks were duly chosen, and each with bated breath
And staring eyes stood watching for the fate much worse than
death.
With outheld palms they stood and watched, when suddenly they
saw
The stick that Joe D'Amato held turned blacker than burnt straw!
The Devil laughed triumphant, the Devil laughed with glee;

"I'm delighted, dear D'Amato! Delighted as can be!"
Then with fraternal gesture he grasped Joe's red suspenders
And in a cloud of sulphur whisked him down to the furnace
   tenders.

VII
Then Joe thought, sad, regretful, of his dear old patron saint,
And all the times he'd said, "He don't," and all the times "I ain't."
And all the commas he'd left out, and semi-colons, too,
And all the words that he'd misspelled; he thought of them with
   rue.
He wished that he had never used a double negative;
He wished that he'd be given just one more chance to live.
"I'll never use bad grammar! I'll never once be late!"
Alas, alack, and woe is him. Too late to change his fate!
So now, down where the fires glow, he cleans the flaming flues
And for all his dreadful English speech, he suffers his just dues.

VIII
Sing yo, ho, ho, and a bottle of beer,
Yo, heave, ho, for the gang's all here.
The gang's all here except for Joe,
'Cause he's in the torrid zone, down below.

Sing hey, nonny-nonny for Carini and Lee,
For they are now married and as happy as can be.
He eats no more white bread, but only dark flour
And he grows healthier, hour by hour.

Sing hey-nonny-nonny for dear old Busie
For he's more famous now than John Philip Sousi.
He plays a grand piano every night on television
With oh! such style! such nuances! such decision!

And a hey-nonny-nonny for Frank Corrao,
As Capra's successor he's the man of the hour!

Yo, ho, ho and a bottle of gin.
Virtue is rewarded, but not so sin.

THE PEN CAN BE AS DANGEROUS AS THE SWORD

When I was working on my graduate degree at the University of Wisconsin, I was still vacillating between the desire to be a writer and the desire to be a psychological counselor. Somehow I became possessed of the idea that the two tendencies could be combined: that one could help people with their psychological problems by writing a poem or a story about them. A dramatization of this kind, I thought, in clear black type on clean white paper, might have a much stronger impact on them than a mere series of counseling sessions could ever have.

It was under the sway of this notion that I began to write a number of pieces for people whom I was trying to help. The following is a faithful account (only the names are changed) of what happened when I wrote a story dramatizing the unbelievable disorderliness of a college friend. Not long afterward, the story was gleefully discovered in a dresser drawer by her husband as he was packing his clothes to leave. He proceeded to give it to his lawyer, who planned to use it as evidence in the divorce proceedings. I must say that this totally unexpected and to me horrifying consequence chastened my views on literary therapy considerably.

Lola was fat, but she was one of the most fascinating people I have ever known. Her amplitude was due principally, I think, to her incurable passion for eating two different kinds of dessert with every meal. As for her fascination, I have often tried to analyze exactly in what it consisted. Beauty was certainly not its principal ingredient.

Her eyes had a kind of Chinese slant, which seemed strangely incongruous in her otherwise Nordic and full-moon face. Her nose was snub, and her chin was bringing up slight reinforcements from the rear. Her only possible claim to beauty was a mass of dark brown hair, which curled in charming tendrils around her neck and temples whenever the weather was damp.

No, her fascination was certainly something distinctly apart from her personal appearance. She was warm and friendly, of course—otherwise, being a rather introverted type myself, I might never have come to know her in the first place. But I have known other warm and friendly people whom I would never describe as being fascinating. Basically it must have been her inexhaustible energy. She was like one of those exuberant, colossal fountains one sees in Rome. Night and day she always seemed to be at the same high pitch of hydraulic power.

Her conversation was inexhaustible, too. She never lacked for something to talk about. When she found the English language to be inadequate, she lapsed—and very cleverly, too—into dialect; she was best at Yiddish, Southern drawl, and British English. When words of any kind seemed insufficient, she pantomimed. Her face was very mobile and she was an excellent mimic.

Perhaps the reason why she always had something to talk about was the close availability of her favorite topic, namely Lola herself. This, according to the ancient definition of a bore as a person who talks about himself when you want to be talking about yourself, should have certainly established her as an insufferable bore. But curiously enough she was seldom if ever boring. At least I did not find her so, in more than a year of close acquaintance, and I have never heard anyone else describe her as such, either. They said other things about her, but never that she was dull company.

It was during World War II, while I was doing graduate work at the University of Wisconsin, that I met her. One evening in September I went to a public lecture and it so happened that she took the seat next to me. At the time I was ever bent on improving each shining minute, so I had brought a book along with me to read: but the hall was too dimly lit to permit reading, and as a consequence the book—a biography of Gandhi, I think it was—lay idly on my lap. Her eye was caught by the title, and she questioned me about it; this naturally led to conversation on other topics, and I soon found myself talking to her as if I had known her all my life. When, after the lecture, she suggested that I come to visit her some time, I promptly agreed. She scrawled her name and address on the margin of the lecture announcement, as neither of us had any paper with us.

I carried it about with me for more than a week before I set out, one afternoon, to look her up. I was rather surprised to find that my scrap of paper had led me to a small and rather shabby apartment building two blocks from the campus called, I believe, the Juniper Apartments or the Westerly Apartments or something equally undistinguished and trisyllabic. For the purposes of this account we had better settle on something definite, so we'll call it the Juniper Apartments.

I entered the unprepossessing building, found the name Wickers on a lobby mailbox, and noted a small sign above it reading: "Bell out of order. Come up and knock." As I mounted the steps to the second floor apartment, I decided to exploit the ambiguity of that quaint invitation at the earliest opportunity. I knocked. A few moments later Lola came and widely opened the door.

"I've come up to knock," I said. "May I?"

"Oh, by all means," she said, cozily taking my arm and leading me in. "My friends knock me all the time. So does my husband." And she laughed her comfortable, diaphragmatic, ever-ready laugh.

It had never occurred to me that she had a husband, so this last sentence came as something of a surprise. She had certainly scribbled the name Lola Wickers, rather than Mrs. Wickers, on the paper; and my impression was that this was how she had introduced herself also. But of course I could have been wrong. During introductions names always slip by me like ships in a fog.

In any case it was perhaps fortunate that she had given me this new frame of reference because just at that moment there toddled into the background a half-dressed infant of about a year and a half. I speak with exactitude. The little girl was literally half-dressed. The upper half. She had curly blond hair and a mischievous little mouth and she was roly-poly like her mother. She announced her presence in a dialect all her own, which Lola apparently understood because she wheeled around and said, "You little scamp. Get back to bed." It was then that I noticed that Lola herself had probably just got out of bed. At any rate, she was wearing a flowered kimono and bedroom slippers.

"Find yourself a place to sit down," she said genially, as she carelessly tucked her offspring under one arm. "I'll have to put Baby to bed for her afternoon nap. She's just as bad as I am. Hates to miss a minute of anything. You know, I still hate to go to bed at night—I'm afraid something exciting might happen and I'd miss it. That's one reason why I would never commit suicide, I guess.' She had reached the bedroom door and had disappeared into it, but she did not stop talking. "You want to know something interesting? I once kept a boy from committing suicide. And you want to know how I did it? Well, it was when I was in college—I went for one semester, you know—and I met this boy in my French class...."

While she was relating this history from the murky interior of the bedroom, I decided to accept her invitation to be seated. It was then that I realized that her remark that I "find a place to sit down" was to be taken literally rather than idiomatically. There were several chairs in the room, but they were covered with books, magazines, boxes, toys, and various articles of clothing. Seven-eighths of the sofa was piled high with what seemed to be odds and ends of a remnant counter. All it lacked was a sign reading Reduced for Clearance. The remaining one-eighth was occupied by two very small kittens, curled up together like two letters of a monogram. A third kitten, I noticed, was washing itself placidly on the windowsill, which was covered with dust. Cat-lover that I am, I could not bring myself to disturb the kittens slumbering on the couch, so I merely stood like a silent sentry in the middle of the room till Lola came back and casually cleared off a chair for me and one for herself.

"...and one night we sat up till about three in the morning. (I must tell you later how I explained it to the housemother. That was a scream!) He was determined to commit suicide the very next day. I had used every argument I could think of and finally I thought to myself, well, what would keep *me* from committing suicide? And then I realized that it would be the thought of all the good food I would miss. I *do* love food, don't you?"

I started to form an affirmative reply, but apparently she had meant it to be a rhetorical question. "So that's what I told him. 'What's your favorite things to eat?' I said. And he told me: 'Irish stew and rice pudding and cranberry sauce with turkey and waffles and potato pancakes and watermelon and cold beer (I remember them so well because they were all my favorites too—all except the potato pancakes) (but I remember telling him I hoped he didn't like them all at the same meal)"—she giggled—"And so then I said, 'Well, if you committed suicide you couldn't enjoy all those things any more, now could you?' Well, you know, that made him stop and think. And he said, 'I guess you're right. And he *didn't* commit suicide after all. I count that as one of my finest accomplishments in life. Would you mind watching me wash the breakfast dishes?"

"Oh, no," I murmured. "I love to watch people wash the breakfast dishes. It's one of my favorite things to do."

So we went into the kitchen. If the living room was disorderly, it was neat as a geometrical figure by comparison with the kitchen. Children's toys and a deck of cards were scattered all over the floor. Cupboard doors were open and half open. Dishes of what must have been two previous meals were stacked in the sink, and the debris of a breakfast serving for five was still on the oil-cloth covered table.

Lola made no apology for the disorder and started leisurely to take the dishes off the table.

"I didn't know you had a family," I remarked, taking advantage of a pin-point of silence.

"Oh, yes. Three children. A boy of seven, a girl of five, and Baby. Didn't I tell you?"

I shook my head. "I didn't even realize you were married."

"Mmmmmmmmmm," she exulted. "You mean I don't have that married look?" She made an expressive grimace and then laughed at herself.

"No. Not conspicuously."

"Well, you see I was married when I was seventeen. The impulsive type. You shall have to meet my husband. Though on the other hand I don't know whether to introduce you or not. You're such a sweet little thing that I don't know if I can risk it." Generous appreciation of her friends was, I came to learn, one of Lola's chief charms.

I do not remember now all the details of the rest of our conversation. I do remember clearly that it was all of two hours before she had cleaned up the kitchen, and in those two hours she had told me the story of how she had acquired the three kittens, and why her husband had insisted that she give away the rabbit, the white mice, and the turtles; a full account of the sensations, physical and emotional, she had experienced when her first child was born; what she thought about spiritualism and life after death; and all her considered opinions on Calendar Reform, the Bahai movement, psychoanalysis, the Book of the Month Club, and whether or not one should eat the whites of hard-boiled eggs. All this had been enlivened by anecdote, fantasy, personal recollection, pantomime, impromptu puns, an occasional quoted (or misquoted) line of poetry, some very bad French, a very good takeoff of a Jewish refugee psychiatrist, and an endless chain of parenthethical and very amusing digressions.

When I left she was insistent that I come back to see her soon. "I've enjoyed talking to you *so* much," she said. She might have added, "Thank you for your kind attention." She couldn't have wanted a more appreciative audience. Her inexhaustibility fascinated me. Listening to Lola talk was like having a front-row seat at a first-rate variety show. I needed no urging to return.

We saw each other frequently thereafter. Since she could not easily leave the baby alone, and since she could not afford a babysitter except for really important occasions, I could not expect her to call on me. So I fell naturally into the habit of dropping in at her place whenever I had an hour or two to spare.

After a few weeks I met her husband, Fred. He worked in a defense plant somewhere and I think he was a mechanic of some kind. His principal passion in life seemed to be driving or otherwise tinkering with his rattletrap car. In appearance he was slender and rather nondescript; in temperament, silent and reserved. Though he seemed amiable enough, he somehow did not seem the proper foil for Lola's exuberance. However, I did not see him often and was not particularly curious about him. Beyond wondering how he could stand the untidiness of the house, and what his reaction to it must be, I did not often think about him.

The fantastic disorder that I had found there on the day of my first visit was, I soon discovered, not one of those domestic accidents that happen in the best of families. It seemed chronic. Occasionally the house was relatively neat, but this never lasted for more than a day or two. Later I discovered that an orderly day signified a visit from Lola's mother or a meeting of her church group or sometimes just an unexplainable eruption of housewifely impulse. I soon learned, too, that they were living in borderline poverty. Besides, the apartment was one of those old-fashioned, high-ceilinged, corniced affairs, which, unless it be smartly furnished and decorated, always look depressingly nineteenth-century and never quite clean. I was able to find excuses for Lola's disorder, though it always repelled me. I would have been ashamed to bring one of my university friends over there, unless they were broad-minded or bohemian enough to be able to appreciate the soul beneath the surface.

Perhaps I should explain before going any further that I have never been outspoken to people about their shortcomings. It has always seemed the safest course to follow, as I have one or two shortcomings of my own. And yet, if ever I had the urge to suggest personal improvement to anyone, it was to Lola about the ungodly mismanagement of her household. The longer I knew her the more it seemed to be growing worse. Still, I probably would never have said anything about it if she had herself not given me the opportunity.

It was about ten o'clock one Sunday night in late October. I had dropped in at Lola's to pick up a book I had left there, and found her in one of her soul-searching moods. Fred and the children were all in bed. Apparently she was feeling lonesome. "Please stay and talk to me," she urged. "Keep your coat on, though. The furnace is out of order. I think I'd better get me a blanket."

So I sat down in an available chair and she sat down opposite me in the middle of the sofa. Except for a few torn magazines, an empty cracker box, and a mound of undarned stockings, the sofa was fairly respectable. Lola sat cross-legged on it, like a Buddhist idol, and wrapped the blanket completely around her. It was an Indian blanket that she had won at a carnival. She started out by telling me the story of how she had won it, and gave a very comic rendition of the conversation between herself and the carnival barker, who was half Armenian and half Irish. But this was not what she really wanted to talk to me about, she explained. What she really wanted to discuss was Lola herself.

Something had happened to upset her usual good spirits. She did not define exactly what it was, but she made veiled allusions to some kind of upheaval which had led her to torturous introspection.

"All day I've been in that 'Why was I born, why am I living?' frame of mind. After today, what? Whither am I tending? You know what I mean?"

I knew what she meant. It was typical of her, even in despondency, not to lose the light touch.

"You know, it's a funny thing," she went on. "After you're married you are sometimes really lonelier than you ever were before." This was the first reference she had ever made to the state of her marriage. "Of course, I've been happy with Fred. But I don't know. Now—Well, I'm dissatisfied with myself somehow. And I think perhaps you can set me straight. So many times I look at my friends and say to myself, 'Now if only she didn't wear that hideous hat; or if only she didn't walk like a poodle; or if only this or only that. I edit people. I might call myself a sort of Human Editor-at-Large. If only they gave Pulitzer Prizes for that sort of thing I could win it easy. What I couldn't do with Louise Sykes, for example! The way that woman talks!" Here followed a brief and deliciousLy accurate characterization of Louise Sykes simpering an order to the grocer over Lola's phone.

"But don't let me talk about Louise Sykes. Because I want you to talk about Lola Wickers. One can never edit oneself, you know. But other people can. And knowing you as I do, I think you're a good editor too. So what do you think about me, please? What should I do to be a better girl?" She grinned, but I could tell that she was very sober beneath the flippancy. She sat silent, waiting for me to say something, and nervously lit a cigarette.

There was something indescribably pathetic and yet indescribably comic about her as she sat there—swathed as she was in the big Indian blanket with only her round, fat face showing solemnly in the midst of it, and surrounded as she was with all the quaint disorder of the living room—a brassiere and a pair of stockings drying to a crisp on the radiator, a stack of movie magazines and a conglomeration of children's toys cluttering the floor at the base of the lamp, the curtains at the window awry, and a white tuft of stuffing bursting out like a cotton boll in bloom from the rip in the sofa.

I savored the comic discrepancies of the situation as I gathered my wits together for a suitable reply. It was not too difficult. I had frequently framed tactful approaches to the matter, which I had never used; here was my opportunity to use them.

"Well," I began judiciously, taking an indirect approach, "I've had the theory for some time now that every one of us has some principal lesson to learn in life."

She nodded assent. "Yes, I think you're right. Go on." She was looking at me with child-like expectancy.

I went on, feeling like the Assistant Dean of Women. "Life is probably like a day in school. All of us have to discover what our lesson for the day really is. It isn't obviously printed on a page, like an assignment in an arithmetic book. Instead it lies deeply hidden within ourselves. Once we discover what our basic defect of character is, we have a clue, I think, to everything that happens to us."

Again she nodded, solemnly. "Yes. Go on."

"For a long time I wondered what my basic defect was. When I finally discovered it, it made the difficulties of my life so much more intelligible and easier to meet."

"You mean you've got a defect?" she said. "It doesn't show."

I acknowledged her flattery with a bow of the head. "Now you make it difficult for me to suggest that you have one."

"Oh, don't feel that way," she said hastily. "I know I do. I want you to tell me what you honestly think."

Feeling like a fully appointed Dean of Women by now I cleared my throat and plunged in. "Well, I think that probably the lesson you have to learn is: 'Order is heaven's first law.'...."

She did not flinch. "Yes. I know what you mean. I'm really not a very good housekeeper, am I?"

"No," I agreed, as gently as I knew how.

Well, we talked for almost four hours. She gave me full reins on the conversation—an exhilarating experience of itself. I expanded on my theme, feeling rather like a combination of Florence Nightingale, bearing a lamp aloft, and Savonarola, crusading nobly against the moral turpitude of his fellowman.

Lola seemed receptive, grateful, penitent, eager to change. When I finally left the house at two a.m., it was with the heady exaltation that a priest must feel after having induced a great conversion. From now on, she had assured me, she was going to try to be different. She put herself in my hands. I had revealed her to herself. Together we would work out a schedule, an orderly way of life, a plan.

Mid-semester examinations kept me preoccupied for a few days and it was late Thursday afternoon before I could stop by to see her again. I mounted the stairs with anticipation. The house would undoubtedly be in order for a change; Lola would be preparing supper with housewifely propriety; and all would be neat and sweet and obeying Heaven's First Law.

How wrong I was. A gayly hallooed *come in* ushered me into the apartment, the weird disorder of which could have equalled only by Dali working in collaboration with a Kansas tornado. Lola was lying on the couch with the sybaritic abandon of a Roman empress, smoking long cigarettes and carrying on one of her interminable telephone conversations. A mound of cigarette butts next to her argued that the session might have been going on for some time.

I wandered into the kitchen—ostensibly for a drink of water, but really to discover the status quo of that particular province of Lola's universe. (I had pointed out with such poetic eloquence that her home was her universe, and she the Lord therein.) Clearly the Lord had abdicated from this portion of His Holy Kingdom also; chaos was on the face of the sink and on the face of the table and floor, too. My image of myself as a redeemer of sick souls shrank. I picked my way carefully over the Tinker Toys and the movie magazines and went back to the living room, where I waited patiently for Lola to finish her telephone conversation.

She was in a particularly scintillating mood, cutting verbal capers like a kitten on a rainy night. Her mimicry had never been so devilish, her puns never so fantastic, her laughter never so like a fountain of champagne. I felt myself growing jealous of whoever it was she was talking to. Her characteristic leisureliness in winding up the conversation made me unreasonably annoyed. Finally I pointed to my watch by way of indicating I had to leave, whereupon she hastily concluded the conversation, hung up the receiver, and without a pause either for breath or apology, began giving me a piquant description of the person to whom she had just been talking.

As usual her characterization held me spellbound, and at 5:30, when I had to tear myself away to keep a six o'clock supper date with a friend, I had not yet found an opening to inquire about her new-found orientation to Life or her newborn Design for Orderly Living. Apparently she had forgotten completely about the whole thing. Once again she was bobbing gaily and buoyantly on the waters of existence.

I went down the stairs, thinking darkly about the futility of trying to change people. Perhaps, after all, hers was the better way. Her disorder was atrocious—but her bubbling joie de vivre was incomparable. Would the world not be a happier place if more people were less orderly and more Lola-like? My gloomy reflections were interrupted when I reached the door and the outside stoop, where Lola's five-year-old daughter Caroline was sitting quietly by herself. Her pretty little face was smudged; the hem of her faded dress was hanging beneath her shabby coat; and a hole in the heel of her stocking showed like a crescent moon. Altogether she looked wistful and neglected; and, thinking of the dirty kitchen upstairs and the unlikelihood of supper being ready for another two hours at least, I felt a sudden pity. We exchanged brief greetings—I did not know her very well—and I went hurriedly on my way.

Until about nine o'clock that night the matter was pushed out of my mind. The moment I left the friend with whom I had had supper, however, and started walking home in the crisp November night, the whole situation arose vividly in my mind's eye once again.

Now I saw it in a different aspect. Before I had thought of Lola's messiness chiefly in aesthetic terms. Now I saw it in human terms. She had joie de vivre, all right, but what about her children? The more I thought about the situation, the more convinced I became that something ought to be done about it. Obviously it was useless to talk to Lola; words spoken today were forgotten tomorrow. But suppose I were to write something about it? Suppose I were to write a story about a fascinating but irresponsible woman who ruined the lives of her children, and showed the story to her? In this way she could see herself objectively. It might startle her into reform.

Plans for the story had already matured by the time I reached my room. By the time I had taken a shower and had a cup of hot chocolate, I had had the brilliant inspiration to write the story, not about some fictitious and vaguely parallel person, but about Lola herself.

At about four in the morning I had completed my little piece of literary psychotherapy. It was only a rough draft, of course; but in the fifty pages I wrote I had created a portrait of Lola exactly as I saw her. I spared no detail. She and Fred and the children were named and described precisely. The disorder of the apartment—located on the second floor of the Juniper apartments two blocks from the University of Wisconsin campus—was completely re-created, down to the minutest detail of undusted furniture, unwashed dishes, unmended bursts in the upholstery, and unemptied ashtrays. The only fictitious thing about it was the dramatic situation I invented.

I created a scene twelve years hence, when Caroline, the little girl, would be seventeen. Fred had just come home from work. A few moments later the doorbell rang and a telegram was handed to him. It was from his sister in Chicago; the message was that Caroline was pregnant and sick, and she—Fred's sister—needed money to help her. Such a situation was to be expected, of course. The girl had been ashamed to bring her friends home, had taken to meeting boys on street corners, and had met up with a handsome university sophomore who had seduced her before dropping out of school and out of sight. Then, discovering her condition and not knowing where to find the father of her unborn child, she had managed to hitch a ride to Chicago to the home of her aunt, with whom she thought she could find refuge since she was afraid to face her very strict father. Fred read the telegram in stunned anguish; then he started looking for Lola. She was nowhere to be found. He called all her friends; no Lola. Finally he went down to the bakery coffeeshop where she frequently went to have a cup of coffee and two desserts with one of her neighbors. And there he found her in a booth, animatedly discussing the state of her soul as she alternately bit into a piece of rum cake on the left side and a six-layer Napoleon on the right.

In the next few days I polished the story, heightened the melodrama and etched more corrosively the descriptive details; then I typed it and bound it in a heavy black cardboard binder, on which I pasted a white index card with the title, *Destiny,* lettered on it in bold India ink. Finally I telephoned Lola and told her I had written a story about her and would she like to see it? But of course! Bring it right over. Feeling somewhat like a redeeming

136

angel I loped over to her house and delivered the story.

I left her place immediately and went home to Milwaukee for the weekend. By Sunday night I began having misgivings about the whole thing, but I dropped over at Lola's none the less on my way home. Lola seemed in a genial enough mood when she opened the door. "Hello, honey," she said when I entered. This reassured me. I gave a quick glance about the room, and barely recognized the place. Curtains which had been hanging blackened and crooked ever since I had first visited her, were now hanging straight and clean; chairs were innocent of clothes and magazines; the floor was uncluttered; ashtrays were empty. I thought it was safe to venture a bit of banter. "Oh, I beg your pardon. I think I've entered the wrong apartment. I thought this was the Wickers' place."

"Quit kidding, brat, and see what I've done." She showed me through the kitchen and the bedroom. The whole house was painfully and unbelievably neat. "I hated you when I first read the story," she said. "Then I cried. Then I re-read it. Then I cried again. But finally I realized I was seeing myself as others see me for the first time in my life. So I decided to do something about it. And I want you to know I appreciate it."

"Oh, that's all right," I murmured, modestly. At least I tried to seem modest. I walked home in a beatific, exhilarated mood. But my exhilaration was short-lived. The house remained neat for about a week. Gradually the effect wore off; and two weeks later the disorder was worse, if possible, than ever before. Lola was in a new mood: defiant, devil-may-care, irresistibly, magnetically gay. I dropped my flag to half mast and decided to confine my efforts at reform from then on exclusively to myself. And that, I thought, was that.

Once again I was wrong. Late one night, about three weeks after I had given her the story, Lola phoned me. I hadn't seen her for almost a week, and was delighted to hear from her. I noted at once that there was an unaccustomed excitement in her voice.

"Gina," she said, "do you know what's happened?" I confessed my ignorance. "Well, Fred has left me. He wants to get a divorce."

I was both surprised and not surprised. I gave the proper expression of dismay and asked, "When did he go?"

"Yesterday morning. But here's the worst of it. He took the story with him. He brought it to his lawyer, and the lawyer said it would make first rate evidence in the trial. Imagine!"

I can't say that my jaw dropped at this announcement, but my state of mind was certainly equivalent to it. "Ye Gods!" I said, using my most forceful expression of chagrin at the time.

Gradually she related the whole story. Fred had been threatening to leave for some time. She hadn't liked to speak of it before, but there it was. Early yesterday morning, while she was out shopping for breakfast rolls and coffee, he had quietly packed his things and left. On returning from the store she found a note on the kitchen table. Later, observing the half empty drawers in the bedroom, she became suddenly fearful about the story. She made a frantic search, only to discover it was gone. That night she had called up his sister's, where she knew Fred would spend the night, and asked him about it. He admitted he had taken the story, and told her that the lawyer had said it was invaluable evidence and would absolutely clinch his case. She pleaded with him to return it; he merely laughed, and said, "Don't hold it against me. Just thank your girl friend for me for having written it."

The news stunned me as much as it did Lola, and in addition made me feel like America's Number One Heel. I told her repeatedly how sorry I was; but she simply said, "You meant well," and "I should have hidden it in a better place," and changed the subject. However, though she never once reproached me for my indiscretion in using actual names, I felt that she was unhappy about it and maybe even resented it. For one thing she didn't phone me very much any more; for another, when I phoned her she seemed depressed and remote and didn't talk very long, which was out of character for her. One day when I had time, I stopped over to see her; but nobody was home. I wasn't able to stop by again because I had three long term papers to write and a lot of research to do. I had the heavy feeling that maybe I had lost a good friend.

November wore on to December. Like all the others whose home was close enough to permit going home for the holidays, I left Madison on the first train out after my last class on a Thursday afternoon. When I returned on the second day of January, my first impulse was to call on Lola and see how she was faring. She greeted me with exuberance. "Darling! I'm so glad to see you! And I've got such wonderful news!"

She was in excellent story-telling form, so it took her a good hour and a half to relate what had happened during my absence. Each detail was painted with vivid verbal brush strokes; each circumstance explained in all its causal relationships; each conversation repeated and interpreted as to its undertones and overtones. In brief, however, the story was this.

A few days before Christmas, Fred had telephoned Lola and asked her if she would care to have him call for her with the car and help her bring home a Christmas tree for the kids. She thought it would be a nice idea, whereupon he duly appeared late that evening, when the children were all in bed. They drove to a Christmas tree lot, selected a brave little spruce, and strapped it to the back of the car. On the way home Fred had stopped at a drug store to pick up some Christmas tree ornaments, and while he was gone Lola decided to smoke a cigarette. She opened the glove compartment to get some matches, and what should she see inside the compartment but Fred's gasoline ration book. Without a second's hesitation she slipped the ration book into her purse, and it was not until the following afternoon that Fred noticed that it was missing.

He called her up that evening. "Lola," he said, "I can't seem to find my gasoline ration book. You didn't happen to notice it last night, did you?" "Yes, darling," she said; "Not only did I notice it, but I've got it. And what's more, I'm going to keep it." "But Lola! I've got to have it! It would take weeks to get another from the board—they're getting very strict and besides the red tape is endless. And there's no way I can get to work without my car. Besides there are five people that I drive there every day."

"Sorry, sweetheart," said Lola, "but you won't get it unless you give me back the story Gina wrote." Fred exploded into profanity. "Dammittall! Don't you know there's a war going on?" "I do, my love, and it's between you and me. And all's fair in love and war. And I intend to get that story back. Pronto. Together with a signed statement that you will not use it in the divorce court."

Well, they argued back and forth for some time and Fred finally realized that he was up against a stone wall. He brought back the story together with the signed statement she wanted the following evening, though he refused to give them to her until she had put the ration book down on one end of the kitchen table, as if in escrow: and she in turn insisted that he put the story and the statement down at the other end of the table at the same time. I wish I could have witnessed the scene.

About six months later, when I had left Madison and gone home for the summer, they got their divorce. The funny part about the whole thing, I thought, was the fact that Lola won the decree, and not Fred. I never knew on what grounds she won it, and whether through fair means or foul, but win it she did, together with the custody of the children and a small but adequate alimony. I understand that she is now happily remarried and also that she is a model housekeeper. All of which leads me to wonder which is mightier, when it comes to reforming a woman's character—the pen, or in some cases at least, the right husband. I must say that my guess inclines me to the latter of the two possibilities. I have therefore unconditionally renounced all efforts at reforming my fellowman or woman through literary means, leaving the laurels in the field on the brows of Rousseau, Tom Paine, and Harriet Beecher Stowe, where they properly belong, anyhow.

TYPEWRITER TROUBLE IN VIRGINIA BEACH

Virginia Beach, years ago, was a quiet little town, not much more than a straight strip of beach with a few hotels, a post office, a drug store, a variety store, some grocery stores, and a cluster of little frame houses set back from the beach on wooded lawns. Now, through annexation and phenomenal growth, it is an enormous sprawl, with high rise hotels, a vast convention center, enormous shopping malls, continuous housing developments, and numerous military installations.

I went there, shortly after getting my Ph.D at the University of Wisconsin, because I had read Sugrue's biography of Edgar Cayce and wanted to investigate the Cayce files concerning reincarnation. It is not true—as rumor persistently has it—that I went there as a skeptic and became a believer. I went there as a person who believed in reincarnation, largely because of a Theosophical background, but who wanted the confirmation of it that the Cayce material promised to provide. I spent two years studying the files, and this research eventually became the two books, Many Mansions *and* The World Within.

Unfortunately, through miscalculating the number of typewritten pages that would make a printed page, I wrote far too much material. The original Many Mansions *was 850 pages long, and when I submitted it to a New York editor he expressed definite interest in publishing it but said that it would have to be cut. (Hugh Lynn remarked, in fact, that if they had published all 850 pages it would have had to be called "The Wheelbarrow Edition.") Cutting it was probably more difficult than writing it; but I finally managed it, condensing things here and cutting whole chapters there. A few years later, when the publisher kept requesting me to do another book, I decided to put together the excluded chapters because they contained such valuable material—on the human body, the glandular system, race, sex, and a philosophy of balance—which were really an integral part of the original manuscript of* Many Mansions. *And so the book was published under the title of* The World Within, *and is currently being reprinted by the Edgar*

Cayce Publishing Company.

The two years I spent at Virginia Beach were fascinating ones, though not without some minor difficulties. Among these were the horrendous humidity in the summer months and the windswept chill of winter. Another minor difficulty proved to be the trouble my old faithful portable Smith-Corona typewriter began to give me. About this I wrote the following piece. It never found a publisher, but it seemed to amuse some of my friends.

It was just last Monday that I first noticed it.

My first thought was that it was just a passing mishap—just a slip of the shift of my typewriter.

Then I found that it happened not only in one, but in every word that had an e in it. The general effect on the page was that of slight but unmistakable inebriation.

At first I was inclined to make light of the whole thing.

I wrote to my friends: "I hope you won't mind my e's standing on tip-toe." Or: "My typewriter seems to have developed a bad case of hiccups." And similar inane pleasantries.

Pleased with the conversational possibilities of the situation, I began to embellish it even more. By Tuesday I was beginning to make studied apologies like: "I do hope you'll forgive the bouncing style my typewriter has just assumed. I do it with e's, of course, but I'm afraid you can't read it with e's...."

On Wednesday, however, I had occasion to reread a page I had written on Tuesday. The general effect was the same sensation I had experienced, at the age of six, when I rode up and down on a horse on a merry-go-round after drinking three bottles of soda pop. It made definitely dizzying reading.

Remorseful now, and feeling genuine concern both for the eyesight and the good temper of my correspondents, I began, on Thursday, to write in a different vein.

"I am eighteen miles from the nearest typewriter repair shop," I wrote (which was true enough), "and so I hope you will bear with me and my typewriter as we zig-zag through life together. I am sorry to subject you to such an awful sentence as this, but...." etc. etc. etc. etc.

It was not until Saturday, however, that I hit upon a really good idea.

"Long ago," I wrote, "I read a story by Edgar Allen Poe in which I discovered that *e* is the most used letter in the English language. This interesting and instructive fact," I continued, "has remained in my subconscious for a long time, but apparently it has just communicated itself through some variety of ESP (Dr. Rhine please note) to the e key on my typewriter. You can see for yourself

142

the unfortunate result. It has developed a very exalted sense of its own importance, a very inflated ego; and as a consequence it refuses to stay on the same level with the rest of the alphabet.

"However," I went on to say, "I really cannot permit the conceit of one letter of the alphabet to interfere with your reading pleasure. So I have decided to substitutx an x for xvxry e I nxxd to usx. I sincxrxly hopx this will bx much morx rxstful on your xyxs than thx pxculiar lxaping xxxrcisx thosx awful e's affordxd."

This novxl solution to thx problxm appxalxd to mx vxry much and I shall probably continux to usx it until somxonx favors mx with a bxttxr suggxstion, or until a cxrtain somxonx pays mx back thx txn dollars hx owxs mx so I can sxttlx my last yxar's dxbt with thx typxwritxr-rxpair man.

OBSERVATIONS AT THE A.R.E.

During my Virginia Beach-Cayce research period, I lived and worked for two years at the old Cayce house (now demolished) by Holly Lake. Edgar Cayce and his wife Gertrude had died before I came, so I never met either of them. After their passing, the downstairs rooms of their home became the headquarters for the Association for Research and Enlightenment (A.R.E.) which had been incorporated to study the Cayce material. The four upstairs bedrooms were rented out to the various workers, volunteers, or visitors who—as a result of an article about Cayce in Coronet *magazine and Thomas Sugrue's biography* There Is A River—*came in a constant stream. So there was always a curious assemblage of compatible and incompatible people there, who made life interesting, to say the least. (To say the most would be another story.)*

Part of the time while I was doing my research I also held the position of editor of the A.R.E. Bulletin. *My desk was next to the front door, and twice a day the postman arrived and laid the mail on my desk. The following piece, printed in the Association newsletter, represents some of the observations I made at the time.*

The United States Postal Service graciously does more than bring us all our members' letters; it also provides the office staff with daily entertainment through the most extraordinary succession of mailmen ever met with outside of a radio comedy show. First there was Mr. A⸺, a genial old fellow with a slightly reddish nose and an inveterate pipe, who expressed a great desire to read books from our library—though he never gave us any more explicit report (after reading them) than to say "very interesting, very interesting indeed." Then there was his successor—a husky young athlete just released from the army, whose interest in spirits had nothing to do with spiritualism, and who often came with the mail bag at a rakish angle and the fragrance of Four Roses or Seagram's on his breath. One day, when the mail had been overdue for at least two hours, we received an unexpected social call on the telephone. It was the mailman. With the mellow voice of inebriation he informed us, quite cordially, that he had some mail for us, but it didn't look very important, so did we mind very much if he didn't bring it till the next day? We were too flabbergasted to say no. His successor was a young chap, also just released from the army, who carried a chip on his shoulder in addition to the mail bag, and was with us for such a few days that we did not have time to discover his personality or become aware of his soul.

The present mailman—with us now for the past four months—is, however, quite a delightful character, and has the unique distinction of being our only mailman in ten months who drinks nothing stronger than Coca-Cola. In addition he has a handsome head of wavy reddish-brown hair which (at my special request, since I have a weakness for wavy brown hair, reddish or no) he occasionally displays by taking off his cap.

His name is David, and he has the charming capacity for making himself perfectly at home wherever he goes. When he delivers the *Saturday Evening Post,* for example, he spreads it open on my desk and reads all the cartoons, from end to beginning, with obvious enjoyment and total disregard for the passing of time. With one wicked crack or another he puts the members of the office force neatly in what he considers their place, and only this morning remarked that the Assassination of Research and Enlightenment was sending out and receiving entirely too much mail to suit him. He was promptly and sternly corrected on the pronunciation of our name, whereupon he remarked that the Association for Research, Enlightenment, and Confusion certainly was doing nothing to enlighten his load—in fact, quite the contrary. At this point we shooed him out of the office and told him never to darken our door again. We didn't really mean it, though. In fact, if we should ever say something to hurt the feelings of all you lovely people and didn't get any mail from you any more, we'd probably sit down and write ourselves a letter, every day of the week, just by way of bringing David back.

PART VI:
FOREWORDS

When I was about eleven years old I decided I wanted to be a writer. The decision changed at least a dozen times in the following years. At different times I knew I wanted to be (among other things) a pianist, an opera singer, a librarian, a psychologist, and an actress. Fortunately I realized in time that I was not temperamentally suited for any of these professions. So eventually I went back to wanting to be a writer.

One of my first efforts at age eleven, when I began to harbor the idea of writing, was to write my own *Forward* to a book about cats that I planned to write. I never really wrote the book, and it came as a great surprise to me when my mother pointed out that the word was spelled *Foreword*. It was my first awakening to the fact that many words are put together in a logical way, with roots or parts that could be used in other words and could form whole families of words, such as, in this case, forehand, forearm, forenoon, forecast. Not only did I never misspell *Foreword* again, but also I became fascinated with the structure of all words—a fascination that has stayed with me ever since.

Later on, when I became known (at least in some circles) as a writer, I was asked to write a number of forewords to other people's books, and the following pieces represent a selection of some of them.

Foreword to Edgar Cayce's WHAT I BELIEVE

Since the appearance of the biography *There Is A River* concerning the extraordinary career of Edgar Cayce, there has been an ever-increasing interest in the personality and work of this simple man who became clairvoyant while he lay asleep in self-induced hypnosis.

His work, of course, lives on in the lives of thousands of people whose health was transformed or lives literally saved by the advice given in his clairvoyant diagnoses. It lives on the readings, rich in medical, psychological, religious, and metaphysical knowledge, which lie in the files of the Association expressly formed to study them.

But a man who has done outstanding work in the world becomes interesting to the public, not only for the work he did, but also as a personality. This is especially the case when he has qualities of magnetism or charm such as to merit the term *personality* in its popular sense of social attraction. Mr. Cayce had such qualities. The warmth, sincerity, generosity, simplicity of heart and of mind have been transferred, to some degree, to the pages of his biography. But the best biographer in the world could not catch the expressiveness of voice, the twinkle of the eye, the humor of the phrase, the frankness of the bursts of temper, the geniality of the whole presence of the man.

People who have read about Mr. Cayce in his biography want to know more about him. The Association for Research and Enlightenment would like to be able to satisfy this very natural curiosity. What is needed, perhaps, is an account of Mr. Cayce written by one who was very close to him in all the years of his psychic activity—by a person such as his secretary, Miss Gladys Davis, or his son, Hugh Lynn Cayce. But they both have been too busy to write that story. And in the meantime people still want to know more about this man, who did the best work of his life while he lay asleep.

The present collection of talks—he himself never cared to dignify what he said with so formal a term as "lecture"—is an effort to satisfy, in part, that human curiosity. For in what a man says we have a mirror which reflects with very little distortion some of the principal features of his mind and heart.

This man was, as we all know, uneducated. He attended nine grades of a county school and was a photographer by trade. His reading was confined almost entirely to the Bible, which he read through faithfully once each year as long as he lived. In later years many people sent him books along the lines of metaphysics and the occult, but he never read the books. He was in the first place too busy to read, and his few hours of relaxation he preferred to spend sitting by the radio listening to Bing Crosby, Seth Parker, or Charlie McCarthy. So his conscious thinking was never that of a trained mind.

But at the same time he was modest. He did not pretend to know more than he actually did know. Most of the illustrations he used to make a point were taken from the book he knew best, the Bible. When he stood up to address the Sunday afternoon audiences that gathered every week at the Cayce Hospital, it was with a full awareness of his academic limitations. Beginning a lecture on the Relativity of Force—a subject suggested by certain metaphysical readings that had been taken—he said: "Many times in a tobacco field I have seen a little worm making a tiny hole in a leaf. From his viewpoint he was doing the very best he could, but he was making an awful mess of the tobacco. I remind myself very much of that worm when I tackle a subject like this."

Combined with this genuine humility as to his intellectual qualifications, and in spite of them, he had a very earnest wish to share what he knew with other people—to exhort and inspire them. Often the logical train of his thought was interrupted as he suddenly saw a propitious opening for words to move, encourage, or awaken his listeners.

It had been the ambition of his youth to become a preacher, and in these talks of his it is plain that he always remained, basically, more of a preacher than a lecturer, more of a counselor

149

than a teacher, more a man of good will than a man of intellect.

And yet his talks are interesting. They do not add much to the store of the world's knowledge, but they serve to arouse interest in the knowledge that is there. They do not cover in an exhaustive or systematic way the field of psychic research, but they do relate some of the personal experiences of a man whose whole life was spent in that field—though to him it was more a human than a scientific endeavor.

It is for their human interest, then, that these six talks of Edgar Cayce are presented to the public that has found his life work important.

Foreword to Richard Calore's book, IN DEFENSE OF CATS

It has been observed in advertising circles, I am told, that the picture of a charming cat on the cover of a woman's magazine will result in an upswing of sales for that particular issue; and that a cat in an advertisement will often have the same gratifying effect for the project in question. I have no way of substantiating this statement; but I would suspect that there is some truth in it, in view of the beauty and impish charm of cats, and in view of their popularity in America today.

And yet despite the vogue that cats are enjoying, the general condition of their species still remains unfortunate. It is somewhat parallel to the status of women. The seductive image of woman is also exploited by advertisers; yet in most countries of the world woman is still regarded as an inferior being and treated very badly, and even in America she does not everywhere have equal opportunities or fair treatment.

Richard Calore is a lover of all animals, as his courageous and eloquent magazine, *The Voice of the Voiceless,* attests. But he has a special dedication to cats, and he has a passionate concern that the suffering to which they are subject be alleviated.

I share Mr. Calore's concern for animals in general and his passion for cats in particular. Like him—and borrowing his very apt borrowing of Will Rogers' line—I never met a cat I didn't like. A house without a cat in it seems to me as incomplete as a house without furniture or drapes. I also share Mr. Calore's indignation against the many cruelties which cats, as well as all other animals, endure. What particularly appalls me is that Christian churches do not take any interest in the problem—as if the inhumane treatment of animals were somehow not their concern, or the suffering of animals not a proper subject for Christian contemplation. Many individual Christians have, of course, been great befrienders of animals both before and after the time of St. Francis; but officially Christian churches have never acknowledged that human beings have any ethical or spiritual obligation to the creatures who so greatly enrich their lives. I cannot remember hearing a single sermon on the subject, or meeting a single clergyman who was not indifferent to the whole matter.

I shall not easily forget an experience I had when I lived in a small coastal town of California, noted for its Spanish heritage and its natural beauty. A little half-grown taupe-grey cat had taken up residence at the front door of the public library. Her choice of a refuge place seemed an intelligent one. Patrons of the library brought her food, and the thick shrubbery near the door provided her with shelter of sorts. But the rainy season was imminent; the nights were cold and damp; and if she had hoped to be adopted by some kindly reader of books, her hopes remained unfulfilled. It was impossible for me to take her, for complicated reasons involving two belligerent anti-cat neighbors which need not be gone into here; but it occurred to me, naively, perhaps, that the pastor of a large and prosperous church across the street would surely be willing to make an announcement to his Sunday congregation about the case. I phoned the church. The official to whom I spoke was indignant at my request. "We are concerned about *people* here," he said sharply, "*not* about animals."

I could not see then, nor do I see now, how one can possibly be concerned about people without also being concerned about how they treat animals. Nor do I see how one can seriously preach the virtues of charity, mercy, and rudimentary Christian kindness without seeing that these virtues cannot be truly virtuous if they stop smugly short to include only our own form of sentient life and exclude all other forms.

And so if Mr. Calore speaks somewhat sharply in this book at times regarding official Christian indifference and apathy in these matters, I cannot but feel that his indignation is justified.

Conan Doyle once wrote: "The greatest danger which can befall a state is when its intellect outruns its soul. It destroyed Atlantis and it may well prove the ruination of our own." If their treatment of animals is any index to the state of people's souls— and I am inclined to think that it is—then I think that Conan

Doyle's statement should be pondered seriously by all of us.

Mr. Calore's informative book will be helpful in making clear what the specific problems are, and some of the things that all of us can do about them.

Foreword to Brad Steiger's KNOW THE FUTURE TODAY: The Amazing Prophecies of Irene Hughes

It gives me particular pleasure to write a foreword to a book by Brad Steiger about Irene Hughes because they happen to be people of whom I am personally very fond, and whom I greatly admire for the excellence of their talents.

Though their talents are quite different, they have certain outstanding qualities in common. They are both scrupulously honest. They are both versatile and wide-ranging in their interests. They both approach psychic matters, one as a writer and the other as a practicing psychic, with unusually careful objectivity.

Careful objectivity is a virtue in many fields, of course, but particularly so in the field of parapsychology, which is still relatively new in the sisterhood of the sciences and still subject to the distortions of wishful thinking, credulity, and carelessness.

I believe it was Allen Spraggett who said that the best attitude with which to approach psychic phenomena is one of *skeptical open-mindedness*. It is an apt phrase, and I quote it often. Both Brad Steiger and Irene Hughes have this attitude.

Brad Steiger—as some readers may know—is the pen name of a former college professor of English. As one might expect, therefore, he writes with unity, coherence, and impeccable syntax over a solid foundation of carefully researched data. But, as one might not expect, there is nothing pedantic or academic in his style. I have not had time to read all of his many books—he is remarkably prolific—but those I have read I have found to be fresh, conversational, entertaining, and well laced with humor. His popularity as a writer is very understandable.

Irene Hughes is already known to a wide public in the Chicago area because she has given exceptionally good psychic counsel to thousands of persons in her office in downtown Chicago, and because she has made some dramatically accurate predictions of natural and international events on her radio and television appearances there. She is known to a wider public through her syndicated newspaper column, which appears in twenty-eight newspapers, and which contains her psychic predictions and advice. But she deserved to be still more widely known, by people everywhere.

I commend *Know the Future Today,* therefore, to any person, veteran or newcomer, interested in the field of the psychic. It includes careful documentation about the past performances of Mrs. Hughes as a prophetess; it offers predictions of the immediate future which bear watching; and it presents a well-drawn portrait of a very lovely lady who is not only a good psychic and an analytical, articulate thinker, but also a concerned and compassionate citizen of the world.

Foreword to LIFE SIGNS—
An Astrological Case Book
The Incredible Files of
Dan Fry
by Mary Jones and Dan Fry

For as long as I have known Dan Fry—some fifteen or sixteen years, I would guess—I have thought that he should some day write a book about his more extraordinary astrological cases. He has always resisted the suggestion—whether from modesty or laziness I was never quite certain, though laziness is not apparent in other non-literary areas of his life. He is notably industrious when it comes to astrological research; and he is untiring in the pursuit of his various cultural interests—Chinese, Russian, and American history, for example, to say nothing of the perfect gin martini and the ultimate gourmet meal. Perhaps, like other persons who have the gifts of wit, humor, and great conversational aplomb, he finds it more to his taste to talk than to write.

In any case, whatever the reason for this long delay, Dan Fry has finally—with some assistance from Mary Jones of Dallas— written a book and I, for one, am glad he did. I must admit that I began as a total skeptic as regards astrology, believing its rationale to be a bit indefensible. Little by little, from personal experience and that of others whom I knew, I found it necessary to revise my views, and I began to look at the subject with curiosity rather than disdain. Now, seeing a collection of Mr. Fry's case histories in print, I cannot help but feel a greater respect than ever before for the validity of this strange science (still called "pseudo" by some), when practiced by a skilled and insightful person.

There is a psychiatrist in Dallas who went to Dan Fry to have his horoscope cast. He gained so much help in the handling of his own neurosis that he has ever since referred patients to him for astrological analysis. I find this indicative not only of Mr. Fry's capabilities, but also of the possible future direction that psychotherapy will take.

Anyone who has the good fortune to be invited to one of Dan Fry's dinner parties soon discovers (amid the greenery of growing plants and the Victorian decor and the over-laden bookshelves) that many of the guests are clients, who have become friends. I find this significant of the affection that Dan bestows—and inspires.

I hope that some day one of these friends will trail him about as Boswell did Johnson, and write the story of Dan Fry himself—Dan Fry the raconteur, the historian, the lover of animals, the humanitarian, the incisive phrase-maker, the astute observer of the human condition, the Anglophile and the Russophile.

In the meanwhile, we can enjoy the present book, catch glimpses of the man through his candid and compassionate case histories, and gain insight into the strange and remarkable way astrology can help us all cope with life—that strange predicament (as William James put it) we all find ourselves in between birth and death.

Foreword to Gladys V. Jones' THE FLOWERING TREE

In every journey there are moments which stand out with peculiar distinctness even after a long passage of time. A cruise that I took through the Mediterranean many years ago has remained with me principally in one vivid memory: the sense of silent exhilaration that came over me as I stood on the Acropolis of Athens and looked, from between classic pillars, downward on land and blue Aegean sea. There was a kind of pure luminosity in the atmosphere and a certain sense of timelessness about the perspective.

I experierienced something of this same feeling when I first read *The Flowering Tree,* and I have reexperienced it every time I have had occasion to pick it up and read a portion of it here or there. The quality of the book is serene, luminous, and timeless, and I believe that it will lift many people from the flat, weary plainlands of daily life into a new and more spacious awareness.

The book is unusual on several counts.

In the first place, while it is not unprecedented for a psychic to write his or her own book, it is really not too common. The psychic gift is not always accompanied by the intellectual capacity for literary production. Usually professional writers write about psychics and their work—as Sugrue wrote about Cayce, for example, and as Stewart Edward White wrote about his wife, Betty. Or psychics write in "collaboration" with a professional writer; or they simply employ a writer to write their book in their name. This, as everyone may know, is referred to as having a ghost writer; and while it seems singularly appropriate for a psychic to use a ghost writer, Gladys Jones did not do so. She wrote this book herself. And not only did she write it, unaided, but she wrote it very well. From the very first pages one has a sense of clear and authentic communication. Whatever Miss Jones had to say she said directly and without clutter. Somehow her own simplicity, honesty, directness, and wisdom have been transmitted to the words she wrote.

As for the substance of this book, I know of nothing in print which is exactly comparable to it. Tacitly accepting the reincarnation idea, without apology or argument, Miss Jones enlarges our understanding of it through her interpretation of the problems of people who have come to her for help. Having seen souls bare before her, and knowing how they have been chastened and mellowed by pain, she gives us in several memorable chapters a healthy and austere reminder that suffering may be a friend, despite its frightening aspect.

But perhaps the most unusual feature of her approach is the symbolic way in which she sees reality. Many psychics whose work I have studied tell me that they see things in symbolic form around their subject. Miss Jones is the only one I know who sees not isolated symbols but a whole sequence of symbols in the form of a myth, a parable, or a fairy story. These stories form a large part of the substance of this book and some of them are quite extraordinary. They are suggestive of the archetypal symbols that one finds in the dream analyses of C. G. Jung. But they are, to me at least, far more interesting, credible, practical, and universally meaningful than any dream analyses I have seen anywhere.

I believe it should be stated that I have known Miss Jones as a close personal friend for many years, and in that period of time she has given symbolic readings for many people known to me as well as a number of them for myself.* From my own experience, then, and from the reports of many others, I know how astonishingly faithful these symbolic sequences usually are to psychological life facts, and also how uplifting and transformative they are to the person receiving them.

This evidential substantiation does not appear in any explicit way in the body of this book, except in one or two small instances; and for this reason it may be disappointing to the rigorous psychic researcher and the skeptic. However, I believe that certain things about her manner of working need to be understood before any

---

*Miss Jones does not read at a distance, but must sit in the presence of the person for whom she is reading.

really fair appraisal can be made.

First of all, I think it should be noted that the clairvoyant does not normally have the same type of relationship with a client as does a psychologist or a psychiatrist. An open discussion of the problem at the outset (which is usual in a psychotherapeutic situation) would in fact invalidate the psychic information, which, by definition, as it were, must be given without benefit of ordinary knowledge. And normally a clairvoyant does not have a frequent or a weekly relationship with a client, so that he does not usually see the client's progress nor share in the good results of his work.

And so, like almost all practicing psychics all over the world, Miss Jones does not keep systematic records or make follow-up studies of her sessions. The client's acceptance or nonacceptance of what he is told becomes apparent in what he says in the course of the reading, or in his general attitude, or in the tenor of the questions that he asks. Thus for the most part Miss Jones knows immediately when her insight is true; and the many people who come to her periodically through the years often relate to her instances of her diagnostic or precognitive accuracy. These confirmations naturally give her assurance as to the validity of her vision; and for her—as for most psychics—this is enough.

Second, it should be noted that, unlike those psychics who can tune in very precisely on mundane matters, such as lost objects, missing persons, murder clues, or the location of oil wells, Miss Jones deals with what for lack of a better term might be called the soul level of reality. Her clairvoyance differs from the usual manifestation of it that it seems to verge on the mystical and visionary. To Miss Jones, as to many mystics, principles are more important that facts, cosmic laws more important than the trivia of daily life, universal values more important than mundane particulars.

Psychologists and parapsychologists may well find this approach technically unsatisfying, but many of them will acknowledge, I believe, if they take time to read this book thoughtfully, that the net result is none the less strangely moving and strangely significant in many ways.

Those who have been interested in the work of Carl Jung will probably be particularly receptive to Miss Jones's approach and quickly note some striking parallels between them. In his autobiography, *Memories, Dreams, and Reflections,* it becomes clear that Jung was a man to whom the soul was a profound reality, and to whom psychic experiences apparently occurred with some frequency. He found it important to relate only the spiritual essence of his life experience, and not the mundane details. He believed that the true life is invisible, and felt that what we are to ourselves and what we appear to other people can be expressed properly only by way of myth.

The Flowering Tree is, I feel, an important contribution to psychological and parapsychological literature. Its sibylline wisdom can do much to restore courage and serenity to human beings caught in the strange and often tragic complexities of twentieth-century life.